73

2739

HOUGHTON MIFFLIN REPRINT EDITIONS

MERCY WARREN
From the Portrait by Copley

COLONIAL WOMEN OF AFFAIRS

WOMEN IN BUSINESS AND THE PROFESSIONS IN AMERICA BEFORE 1776

BY

ELISABETH ANTHONY DEXTER, Ph.D.

SECOND EDITION, REVISED

AUGUSTUS M. KELLEY • PUBLISHERS
CLIFTON 1972

First Published 1931

(Boston: Houghton Mifflin Company)

Copyright 1924, 1931 by Elisabeth Anthony Dexter

RE-ISSUED 1972 BY

AUGUSTUS M. KELLEY · PUBLISHERS

Clifton New Jersey 07012

By Arrangement with HOUGHTON MIFFLIN COMPANY

Library of Congress Cataloging in Publication Data

Dexter, Elisabeth Williams (Anthony) 1887-
    Colonial women of affairs.

    (Houghton Mifflin reprint editions)
    "Second edition, revised."
    Reprint of the 1931 ed.
    Bibliography: p.
    1. Women in the United States. 2. United States--
Social life and customs--Colonial period. I. Title.
E195.D52 1972   331.4'0973   71-153180
ISBN 0-678-03569-5

PRINTED IN THE UNITED STATES OF AMERICA
by SENTRY PRESS, NEW YORK, N. Y. 10013

TO

MEMORY AND HOPE

MY MOTHER

HARRIET WYATT (ANGELL) ANTHONY

AND

MY DAUGHTER

HARRIET ANGELL DEXTER

PREFACE TO THE SECOND EDITION

AN author who reads his own book after a lapse of years is bound to question it closely. Can he still agree with it? "Colonial Women" was a pioneering effort for me. Since it was written, I have learned somewhat more about the position and activities of women, in other times and places, but the picture I have drawn of colonial America still seems to me substantially true. Two or three errors of detail have been corrected, and some new material added in supplementary "Notes." Except in one respect, it has not appeared needful to alter my conclusions, most of which were then and still are tentative. Although I know more about certain legal handicaps which existed for colonial women, these did not ordinarily, I think, affect their freedom within limits as I have presented it.

Comparisons, if not always odious, appear to be instinctive, and usually dangerous. In 1924, I suggested that possibly conditions for women, in some respects at least, were more favorable in colonial days than they became in the early nineteenth century. I am now considerably more confident that this was the case. Yet, since all knowledge is tentative, it has seemed as well to leave the hypothesis as originally written. The reasons offered in explanation I still think true as far as they go. I hope to have more light on this point some day, and to develop it further.

The preceding conclusion was advanced with fear and trembling — I suppose because it went counter to the usual assumption. Another (implied) comparison, regarding the status of women in the United States and in other countries, was offered without any searchings of heart, because it was in harmony with the usual assumption. I now know enough to realize my ignorance of too much which any such comparison involves, and the sentences dealing with it have been omitted.

When the book first appeared, I was somewhat amused, and a little disturbed, because several critics welcomed it as in some sense an attack on the modern women's rights movement. Careful rereading, however, has left my conscience clear. If the interpretation was based on my statement that colonial women, unlike modern ones, did not blazon their achievements, I would add that men also have learned a good deal about publicity, and that to-day "It pays to advertise" is Axiom the First. Or is the fact that women of two centuries ago showed considerable independence an argument

PREFACE TO THE SECOND EDITION

against women's possessing somewhat more independence now? It would seem rather that the faint-hearted might be cheered to learn that society had shown itself able to survive so much strain. A large proportion of the women presented were married, and had children; it does not appear that any of their activities, from writing poems to keeping a tobacco shop, injured their family life. My hope is that modern women may show as much courage in meeting the problems of the present, and that women and men, together, may go forward.

ELISABETH ANTHONY DEXTER

CAMBRIDGE, MASSACHUSETTS
January 9, 1931

PREFACE

ONE of the pleasantest features of a task like mine has been the constant kindness received from busy people of diverse sorts, whose varying interests touch mine at some particular point.

My first thanks are due to my cousin, Margaret Bingham Stillwell, Curator of the Annmary Brown Memorial, Providence. The idea of writing this book grew out of a conversation with her, and she encouraged me to undertake the research. She has given constant evidence of her interest, and I owe her a particular debt of gratitude in regard to the illustrations; considerably more than half of those presented here were obtained by her, at no small cost of time and effort.

The largest single source of information, as the reader will discover, was colonial newspapers, and I was fortunate in having access to the admirable collection of the American Antiquarian Society, in Worcester. I am under obligations to each member of its staff, in particular to Mr. Clarence S. Brigham and to his associate, Mrs. Reynolds. Mr. Brigham read my manuscript, and gave me helpful suggestions at every stage of my work. He has aided me also in securing illustrations.

PREFACE

The Worcester Public Library was of great assistance, and I am indebted to the staff of the Reference Department there — particularly to my friend Miss Maude E. Wesby.

Dr. George Hubbard Blakeslee, of Clark University; Dr. Harry Elmer Barnes, of Smith College; Mrs. William T. Forbes, of Worcester; and Mr. Howard M. Chapin, of the Rhode Island Historical Society, Providence, gave me suggestions, criticisms, and encouragement, for all of which I am deeply grateful.

The arduous search for illustrations was lightened by the uniform kindness and helpfulness of those who were approached in this undertaking. Mr. George Francis Dow, of the Society for the Preservation of New England Antiquities, was particularly generous and helpful. I wish also to thank Mr. George Parker Winship, of the Widener Memorial Library, Cambridge; Mr. Lawrence C. Wroth, of the John Carter Brown Library, Providence; Mr. John R. Hess, of the Editorial Staff of the *Providence Journal;* Mr. Harry L. Koopman, of the John Hay Library, Providence; Colonel George L. Shepley and Mr. Norman M. Ishman, of Providence; Mr. Worthington C. Ford, of the Massachusetts Historical Society, Boston; and Mr. Henry W. Belknap, of Essex Institute, Salem.

PREFACE

It is becoming almost a commonplace for an author to express thanks to husband or wife. I sometimes wonder how any unmarried person ever succeeds in writing a book! Who else can be trusted to give absolutely honest criticism, unsugared by one bit of flattery? And who else never loses interest, and day by day encourages a sometimes flagging muse? For his unremitting helpfulness, sympathy, and patience, I thank my husband, Robert Cloutman Dexter.

ELISABETH ANTHONY DEXTER

SARATOGA SPRINGS, NEW YORK
March 21, 1924

CONTENTS

ILLUSTRATIONS

ILLUSTRATIONS

INTRODUCTION

Few more fundamental questions confront modern society than what should be the function of women in the work of the world. The answers vary according to the time, the place, the economic condition, the religious and social convictions of the writer. The battle has raged fiercely over these answers, and although some aspects of the question now appear to be settled — practically if not theoretically — other aspects are as much the subject of controversy as ever.

It is not only the practical applications of this question which have drawn blood; the battle has been waged just as vigorously over what *were* the facts at different periods of the past as over what they should be now. The woman of the prehistoric age, for instance, has aroused an amount of discussion which would have astounded that probably unspeculative person.

In the midst of the clamor, however, one period has apparently remained undisturbed, the horror of the "suffragettes," the haven of the "antis." No one has ever denied that the woman of colonial America worked. She has been extolled and pitied

INTRODUCTION

for her devotion and endurance in sharing her husband's toil of clearing the land and running the farm, while she carried on an appalling list of "household industries": making clothes for the family out of wool or flax which she had raised, spun, dyed, and woven; brewing, baking, curing, dipping candles; and meanwhile bearing and rearing, and according to her own attainments educating, a baker's dozen of children. The list seems indeed sufficient. But alter it as one might, every one has agreed that in colonial days woman's place *was* in the home.

The tradition has not been seriously questioned. So careful a sociological writer as Miss Edith Abbot says: [1]

A detailed survey of the field of employment for women during this earlier period is impossible because of the scarcity of records. Moreover, such a study would be on the whole unprofitable.

Historians of the colonial period have been aware, of course, of some outstanding exceptions to this distinctly domestic rôle of women, but they may very reasonably have assumed from the words of Governor Winthrop that such exceptions were indeed neither common nor approved. The passage from Winthrop carries the more weight as he is

[1] Abbot, p. 1.

INTRODUCTION

known to have been the devoted husband of a very
competent and lovable wife: [1]

Mr. Hopkins, the governor of Hartford upon Connecticut, came to Boston, and brought with him his
wife, a godly young woman and of special parts, who
was fallen into a sad infirmity, the loss of her understanding and reason, which had been growing upon
her diverse years, by occasion of her giving herself
wholly to reading and writing, and had written many
books. Her husband, being very loving and tender of
her, was loth to grieve her; but he saw his error when
it was too late. For if she had attended her household
affairs, and such things as belong to women, and not
gone out of her way to meddle with such things as are
proper for men, whose minds are stronger, etc., she
had kept her wits, and might have improved them
usefully and honorably in the place God had set her.
He brought her to Boston, and left her with her
brother Mr. Yale, a merchant, to try what means
might be had for her here. But no help could be had.

Notwithstanding this discouragement from the
sociologist, and this awful warning to female book-
writers by a member of the sex "whose minds are
stronger, etc.," the writer has had the temerity to
investigate the subject. This study offers no answer to the question with which this Introduction
began. It is far from being a complete answer even
to the question, "What, outside of their homes, did
colonial women do?" It is concerned less with the

[1] Winthrop, vol. II, p. 265.

work itself, or with the remuneration received, than with these as evidences of independence and initiative on the part of women, and with the acceptance of these qualities by society. Consequently it touches lightly or not at all upon certain kinds of workers who are important from other angles, as, for instance, domestic servants and saleswomen; and it goes into detail regarding other women who may have worked without pay, or thought of pay, such as some of the writers and religious leaders.

If the following pages succeed in some degree in showing how some of our ancestors met the ever-present problems of women's place in the economic and social life of their time, it will have fulfilled its purpose. Should it fail in this undertaking, it may still, perhaps, help us to appreciate more fully the human qualities of the women of a by-gone generation.

COLONIAL WOMEN OF AFFAIRS

COLONIAL WOMEN OF AFFAIRS

∵

CHAPTER I

MY HOSTESS OF THE TAVERN

FALSTAFF: And is not my hostess of the tavern a most sweet wench?
King Henry IV, Part I, Act I, Sc. 2.

THE woman tavern-keeper was a familiar figure in
Elizabethan England. Soon after the settlement,
she became equally familiar in the colonies, although hostesses resembling Mistress Quickly
would hardly have been tolerated. At a surprisingly early date the town selectmen and the
General Courts were making sure that every town
contained an ordinary, as the inns of the time
were appropriately named. If none of the good
fathers felt a call to become an innkeeper, the
selectmen would choose one who had a large and
conveniently located house, and deliver the call to
him direct.

The standards of what constituted a "large and
conveniently located house" were not unduly high.
As late as 1768 Mary Austin, of Stanwich, Connecticut, advertised for sale a house two stories

1

high, forty-five by thirty feet, four rooms on a floor, saying: [1]

It is very conveniently situated for a merchant or tavern keeper, and is much noted, as there has been a mercantile store and tavern there for some time, and neither merchant nor tavern within four miles.

Under these conditions it is easy to understand why innkeeping for women was advantageous. A woman who found herself deprived of support by the death of husband or father, whose chief legacy must in many cases have been the homestead, could find no readier means of maintaining her home than that of entertaining travelers. All the evidence indicates that women constituted a larger proportion of the hotel-keepers then than they do now.

These hostelries were of all types, from that of the woman who merely consented to rent a room and furnish meals on demand, to that of the hostess whose excellent tavern was known for miles around. There, travelers betook themselves gladly, the judges on circuit made a point of dining, and groups, such as proprietors of townships, held their regular meetings.

The assistance of a man must often have been desirable, especially when — as was always the

[1] *New York Mercury*, January 18, 1768.

case in an enterprise of any importance — the license to keep the inn included the privilege of "drawing wine." One early case shows the interest taken by the court in every detail. Records of the Quarterly Courts of Essex County for 1647 state that on petition of Mrs. Clark, of Salem, widow, she was licensed to keep the ordinary there, with liberty to draw wine, for which privileges she was to pay a fee of ten pounds annually; all, however, on condition that she "provide a fitt man y[t] is godlie to manage ye business," he to be approved by the General Court.[1] Apparently Mrs. Clark and her "godlie" bartender prospered.

The record of another woman appointed by the Essex County Court is less satisfactory. In April, 1666, Elizabeth Sharrat (Sherrod?) was licensed to keep the ordinary at Haverhill for the ensuing year.[2] In October, 1667, Thomas Mudgett sued Hugh Sharrat and wife Elizabeth for not paying for a pipe of wine and other goods delivered to the said Elizabeth in May, 1666;[3] the court found for the plaintiff, and Elizabeth's license was never renewed.

In October, 1704, Madam Sarah Knight, of Boston, traveled on horseback from Boston to New Haven, and thence to New York, returning in

1 *Quarterly Courts of Essex County*, vol. I. p. 123.
2 *Ibid.*, vol. III, p. 319.   3 *Ibid.*, vol. III, p. 450.

March, 1705. Madam Knight will be considered in a later chapter, but testimony regarding the inns of the day may be found in the diary which she kept on her journey. For part of the journey she found fellow travelers, and for other parts she hired a guide. She went first to Dedham, where she stopped to see friends, and then: [1]

to ye tavern, where I hoped to get my guide, and desired the Hostess to inquire of her guests whether any of them would go with mee. But they being tyed by the Lipps to a pewter Engine, scarcely allowed themselves time to say what clownish. . . . [half page of text missing] Pieces of eight, I told her no, I would not be accessary to such extortion.

Then John shan't go, sais shee. No indeed shan't hee; and she held forth at that rate a long time, that I began to fear I was got among the Quaking tribe, beleeving not a Limbertong'd sister among them could outdo Madam Hostess.

Upon this, to my no small surprise, son John arrose, and gravely demanded what I would give him to go with me? Give you, sais I, are you John? Yes, sais he, for want of a better. — Well, Mr. John, sais I, make your demands. Why, half a piece of eight and a dram, sais John. I agreed and gave him a Dram (now) in hand to bind the bargain.

My hostess catechis'd John for going so cheep, saying his poor wife would break her heart.

During the journey Madam Knight stopped at a

[1] Madam Knight's *Journal*, p. 19 ff.

diversity of inns, good and bad, some kept by men, and some by women. The next kept by a woman was on the road to Westerly, Rhode Island.[1]

... Arriving at an Ordinary about two miles further, found tollerable accomodation. ... But our hostess, being a pretty full mouth'd old creature, entertained our fellow traveler, the doctor, with Inumerable complaints of her bodily infirmities; ... But poor weary I slip out to enter my mind in my Jornal, and left my great Landlady with her Talkative Guests to themselves.

A day or two later, she mentions "being safely arrived at the house of Mrs. Prentice in New London." [2] The editor's note says that this was the third wife, and widow, of John Prentice, who died in 1691. His widow kept a well-known inn for many years.

Farther on her journey, beyond the Niantic River, Madam Knight [3]

came to an ordinary, were well entertained by a woman about seventy and vantage, but of as sound Intellectuals as one of seventeen. She entertained Mr. Wheeler with some passages of a wedding awhile ago at a place hard by, the bridegroom being about her age or something above, Saying his children were dredfully against their father's marrying, which she condemned them extremely for.

[1] Madam Knight's *Journal*, p. 38.
[2] *Ibid.*, p. 44.   [3] *Ibid.*, p. 46.

A little instance of class solidarity, perhaps. As Madam Knight was then a widow, although only thirty-eight years old, and as she never changed her condition, she may have been less sympathetic with the aged bridegroom than was the hostess.

The next landlady encountered was less to Madam Knight's taste. At Saybrook Ferry,[1]

Landlady came in, with her hair about her ears, and hands at full pay, scratching. Shee told us shee had some mutton wch shee would broil for us, wch I was glad to hear: But I supose forgot to wash her scratchers; in a little time she brot it in, but it being pikled and my guid said it smelt strong of head sauce. We left it, and paid sixpence apiece for our Dinners, which was only smell.

Better fortune awaited the poor traveler at Norwalk, where the hostess served [2] "a dinner of fryed venison, very savory."

Some years later, when living in Connecticut, Madam Knight herself maintained an inn on the Norwich road. One can feel quite certain that the guests there did not suffer some of the hardships which their hostess had encountered.

The first newspaper in the New World, the "Boston Newsletter," was started the same year that Madam Knight took her journey to New

[1] Madam Knight's *Journal*, p. 48 ff.   [2] *Ibid.*, p. 62.

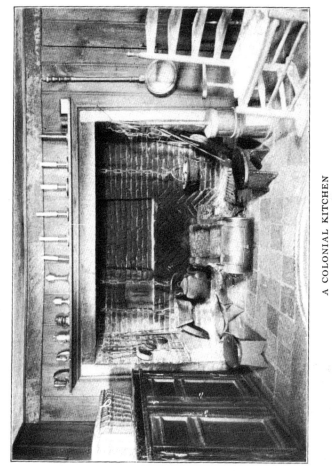

A COLONIAL KITCHEN

(In the House of the Seven Gables, Salem)

MY HOSTESS OF THE TAVERN

York. Direct advertisements by hotel-keepers were rare for another fifty years, but evidence of many taverns soon appeared, through the notices of vendues, meetings of creditors, proprietors of townships, and so forth, which were customarily held at the most convenient tavern. Other occasions for newspaper publicity were sales, settlements of estates, and removals, as for instance: [1]

All persons who are indebted to Anne Jones at the Plume of Feathers in the Second Street in Philadelphia are desired to come and Settle the same, and those to whom she is indebted are desired to bring in their Accounts in order to be adjusted. She likewise designs to dispose of the Lease of her House, as also all sorts of Household Goods at reasonable Rates, she designing to go for England in a short time.

The inns played their part in the excitements and mysteries of the times, and notices like the following were not infrequent: [2]

If anyone can give any account of the Right Heir of One Isaac Taylor that came from Concord in New England Thirty years since or thereabouts to Ponapon in the Parish of St. Paul's in South Carolina, let them enquire at Mrs. Holm's at the Bunch of Grapes in Boston, for a letter.

The colonists were always interested in expand-

[1] *American Mercury*, June 27, 1723.
[2] *Boston Evening Post*, September 14, 1729.

ing their territory, and grants of land were often made as a reward for military service. Townships were promptly organized on such land — at first, often, merely on paper — and the proprietors held meetings, annually or oftener. A popular place for these and similar functions appears in the following notice, published in September of 1740: [1]

These are to Notify the Proprietors of Soughegan West (number 3) that there will be a Meeting of said Proprietors at the House of Mrs. Margaret Pratt, Innholder, in Salem, on Tuesday the 7th of October next, at nine o'clock before Noon.

These proprietors and the proprietors of the "Salem Canada Township"[2] continued to meet at the Ship Tavern, as Mrs. Pratt's house was named, from 1740 or 1741 until 1765. Captain Francis Goelet, of whom more anon, mentions putting up his horses at the Widow Pratt's, while he walked about the town, in 1750.[3] A notice regarding the settlement of Margaret Pratt's estate appeared in 1766.[4] A Mrs. Adams kept a tavern in Salem about the same time, as a house for sale in 1770 is described as opposite Mrs. Adams's tavern.[5]

1 *Boston Evening Post*, September 8, 1740.
2 *Ibid.*, August 16, 1741.
3 *New England Register*, vol. 24, p. 57.
4 *Boston Evening Post*, March 10, 1766.
5 *Essex County Gazette*, December 11, 1770.

MY HOSTESS OF THE TAVERN

The names of the ancient inns were often picturesque; among those kept by women may be found, besides, Mrs. Jones's "Plume of Feathers," "The Royal Standard" (Rebecca Pratt),[1] "The Blue Anchor" (Widow Withy),[2] "The Conestoga Waggon" (Mary Jenkins),[3] "The Fountain and Three Tons" (Mary Yeats),[4] "The Three Mariners" (Margaret Berwick),[5] "The Rose and Crown" (Margaret Ingram)[6] — all these in Philadelphia. In 1762, Sarah Raunall of the same place published the following:[7]

The subscriber begs leave to inform the Public, that she has removed from the Sign of the Siege of Louisbourg, a little below the drawbridge, Philadelphia, to the House where Mr. Murry kept the Sign of the Salutation Tavern, upon Society Hill, and next door to Mr. Neiman's, where she has a very commodious House, fit to entertain a large company of Gentlemen; likewise a very good Billiard Table.

Apparently ladies did not yet constitute an important part of the traveling public; but that the conception of what constituted proper entertainment was broadening, the billiard table testifies.

The vendue, as an auction was generally called,

[1] *Pennsylvania Gazette*, June 5, 1755.
[2] *Ibid.*, March 17, 1768.   [3] *Ibid.*, July 14, 1768.
[4] *Ibid.*, May 30, 1771.   [5] *Ibid.*, March 30, 1738.
[6] *Ibid.*, September 27, 1748.   [7] *Ibid.*, September 23, 1762.

was an important and frequent event in colonial life. Real estate, usually of such undeveloped land as has just been referred to, and used household goods, or the stock of a shop which was closing out, were the most frequent objects of sale; but regular merchants' goods were sometimes disposed of in this manner. In times of war, particularly during King George's War, 1740–48, and the Seven Years' War, 1756–63, excitement and profit were added to colonial life by the sale at auction of prize cargoes from French ships captured by privateers. All seaport towns have records of these dashing days. Vendues were commonly held at taverns. During part of 1758 and 1759, auction sales of "a very good assortment of European goods" were held weekly at the King's Head Tavern, Boston — Widow Davenport, proprietor.[1]

Apparently the Widow Lawrence kept a nautical tavern in New York, for a "Publick Vendue" of the cargo of prize ships was frequently held at her house "on the New Dock." In August, 1747,[2] the ship also was to be sold there; in the following June,[3] two prize ships and cargoes were on sale. An advertisement in August, 1748,[4] is more explicit:

---

[1] *Boston Evening Post*, December 4, 1758 and ff.
[2] *New York Gazette*, August 24, 1747.
[3] *Ibid.*, June 20, 1748.   [4] *Ibid.*, August 29, 1748.

MY HOSTESS OF THE TAVERN

A Parcel of Maracaibo and Caraccas Cocoa, Flour,
Wheat, Steel, Earthen Ware, Glass, Soap, Tallow,
Skins, Hats, Silks, Silver and Gold Lace, Drugs for
Apothecaries and sundry sorts of other Goods.

As the peace of Aix-la-Chapelle was signed on
October 18, 1748, it is to be hoped that the
prize ship which Mrs. Lawrence advertised on
October 10, 1748, was a last effort.

Although the newspapers were printed in only a
few of the larger towns, notice of meetings and of
vendues were of widespread interest, so that the
papers chronicled those held not only in the place of
publication, but in outlying towns. Taverns, also,
were of greater importance to the possible traveler
in another town than to the near-by dweller. Consequently we have more information about inns
throughout the colonies than is the case regarding most other kinds of business. The New York
papers contained advertisements or notices regarding "The King's Arms"[1] in Albany, Martha Vernor, proprietor; another house in Albany kept by
the Widow Brett;[2] and "The Duke of Rutland,"
in Elizabethtown, Mrs. Johnson, proprietor.[3] The
Philadelphia papers mentioned "The Clothiers's
Arms," in Bristol, kept by Mary Jackson,[4] and

[1] *New York Gazette*, July 6, 1765.
[2] *Ibid.*, November 28, 1748.   [3] *Ibid.*, June 27, 1768.
[4] *Pennsylvania Gazette*, June 5, 1755.

COLONIAL WOMEN OF AFFAIRS

Susannah McLaughlin's tavern in Fredericktown, Maryland.[1] The "Boston Evening Post" catered extensively to the provinces, and gave publicity to the inns of Mrs. Abigail Jarvice in Roxbury,[2] Mary Perkins in Gloucester,[3] Ann Slayton[4] and Elizabeth Pike[5] in Portsmouth, Sarah Cutler in Weston,[6] Dorothy Coolidge in Watertown,[7] Yetmercy Howland in Bristol,[8] and Rebecca Wetherell in Plymouth.[9]

Around the middle of the eighteenth century, the idea gained credit that inns might be used for something else than the necessities of travel, and that they might have something more than the "comforts of home"; there is reason to fear that all too often in the earlier days they had had much less. A coffee house was first established in England in 1652, but the earliest use of the term noticed in the colonies was in 1745 — Widow Roberts's Coffee House in Philadelphia. The following advertisement in the "Boston Evening Post" has an attractive ring:

For the Entertainment of Gentlemen, Benefit of

[1] *Pennsylvania Gazette*, May 19, 1763.
[2] *Boston Evening Post*, April 8, 1751.
[3] *Ibid.*, January 6, 1755.   [4] *Ibid.*, May 26, 1755.
[5] *Ibid.*, April 15, 1742.   [6] *Ibid.*, January 4, 1762.
[7] *Ibid.*, February 20, 1775.   [8] *Ibid.*, April 2, 1744.
[9] *Ibid.*, May 7, 1744.

MY HOSTESS OF THE TAVERN

Commerce, and Dispatch of Business, a Coffee House is this day opened in King Street. All the Newspapers upon the Continent are regularly taken in, and several English Prints and Magazines are ordered. Gentlemen who are pleased to use the House, may at any Time of Day, after the manner of those in London, have Tea, Coffee, or Chocolate, and constant Attendance given by

their humble Servant
MARY BALLARD

BOSTON
December 8, 1755

Just this combination of physical and intellectual comfort is hardly available to the general public to-day. The British Coffee House, as it was called, must have been a success, as it is often mentioned. If Mrs. Ballard had a taste for romance, she had opportunity to gratify it, if we may judge from the following: [1]

To the Ladies

Any young Lady, between the Age of 18 and 23, of a middling Stature; brown Hair; regular features, and with a lively brisk eye; of good morals and not tinctur'd with anything that may sully so distinguishable a Form; possessed of 3 or 400 pounds entirely at her own Disposal, and where there will be no necessity of going through the tiresome Talk of addressing Parents or Guardians for their consent; such a one, on leaving a line directed for A. W. at the British Coffee House in King-street appointing where an

[1] *Boston Evening Post*, February 26, 1759.

13

Interview may be had, will meet with a Person who flatters himself that he shall not be thought disagreeable by any Lady answering the above Description.

N.B. Profound Secrecy will be observ'd. No trifling Answers will be regarded.

It is tantalizing not to know whether any young lady felt that she answered the above description; and if so, whether indeed she found the modest young man not disagreeable.

If the young ladies of Boston could only leave love letters at the British Coffee House, the damsels of Providence were soon to be better accommodated.

The "Providence Gazette" for March 9, 1765 gave notice of this forerunner of the automobile inn:

For the Convenient Reception and Entertainment of Gentlemen and Ladies, whenever they are disposed to recreate themselves by an Excursion into the Country, whether at Morning or Evening,
On Monday next will be open'd by
Abigail Williams,
At the Sign of the White Horse, (the House of Jeremiah Williams, Cranston)

THE RURAL TEA AND COFFEE HOUSE

Very pleasantly situated about three miles from the Town of Providence, on one of the most delightful Roads in New England.

MY HOSTESS OF THE TAVERN

Those who are pleased to favour her with their Company may depend on the best of Entertainment, and the civilest Usage, as it will be her Constant Endeavour to deserve a continuance of their Favour.

N.B. Travellers may be genteely accomodated at the same Place.

If the performance was at all equal to the promise, Abigail Williams should have done a thriving business. The charms of a leisurely drive for three miles through the country between Providence and Cranston, are among the pleasures which have gone forever, along with the "Sign of the White Horse."

The bulk of our information about the eighteenth century comes from the newspapers; but more intimate glimpses of life then are afforded by some of the diaries which, fortunately, were commonly kept in those days. Many of these diaries are uninteresting accounts of sermons and funerals, but others are sufficiently vivacious. Two which have been preserved give distinctly unpuritanical accounts of Boston and Philadelphia, respectively. The latter was written by Jacob Hiltzheimer, a German immigrant who had married into one of the Quaker families, and it runs from 1765 to 1798. Hiltzheimer was an excellent man in every sense, but his conscience did

15

not ban all pleasure. On October 17, 1769, he mentions a pleasant evening spent with ten friends at the house of the Widow Jenkins (the mistress of "The Conestoga Waggon," undoubtedly.) On March 16th, following, the Amicable Fire Company, to which he belonged, met at Widow Jenkins's. Under the date of November 23, 1772, he wrote:

This evening went to the Widow Spence's; there supped on venison with the following gentlemen: [four names] Jacob Bates gave the supper on account of leaving the city for Carolina.

On December 28th he tells how he and some friends spent "the forepart of the evening," and then "went to Mary Jenkins and had supper at one o'clock."

The author of the Boston diary, Captain Francis Goelet, of New York, merchant, spent the autumn of 1750 in Boston and vicinity, while his vessel was under repair. He was probably a younger man than Hiltzheimer, and he paints a very rosy picture of the pleasures of society in the Hub. He was a guest of the Wendells, and he takes pains to state that the company, on the various outings in which he disported himself, were the first people in town. There were dances, whist parties, and rides to nearby towns for supper. A friend of his, also a seafaring man, was staying at the tavern kept by one Mrs. Grace. Captain Goelet wrote with more vigor than correctness, and it is sometimes difficult to make out all his meaning; the peculiarities in the following narrative may be accounted for, if it was written "the morning after": [1]

Nov. 5, Being now all ready to Sale, I determined to pay my way in time, which I accordingly did at Mrs. Grace's at the Request Mr. Heylegher and the other Gentlemen Gave them a Good Supper with Wine and arack Punch Galore, where Exceeding Merry, Drinking Toasts Singing roareing, &c., untill Morning when Could Scarce see One another being blinded by the Wine Arack &c. We were ab^t 20 in Comp^y.

Poor Mrs. Grace! One hopes that the "roareing" was not forgotten in casting up the hearty captain's account.

[1] *New England Register*, vol. 24, p. 61.

CHAPTER II

THE "SHE–MERCHANT"

THE reading public of New York, in 1733, must have had its attention attracted by the following letter:[1]

MR. ZENGER,

We, the widdows of this city, have had a Meeting, and as our case is something Deplorable, we beg you will give it Place in your *Weekly Journal*, that we may be Relieved, it is as follows.

We are House keepers, Pay our Taxes, carry on Trade, and most of us are she Merchants, and as we in some measure contribute to the Support of Government, we ought to be Intituled to some of the Sweets of it; but we find ourselves entirely neglected, while the Husbands that live in our Neighborhood are daily invited to Dine at Court; we have the Vanity to think we can be full as Entertaining, and make as brave a Defence in Case of an Invasion and perhaps not turn Taile so soon as some of them.

No information is forthcoming as to the numerous allusions contained in this epistle; and it is quite possible that the editor, John Peter Zenger, who was an enterprising journalist with a sense of humor, may have helped the widows out by writing

[1] *New York Journal*, January 21, 1733.

this letter for them. In any event, however, it is good evidence that the woman shopkeeper was a recognized member of New York society.

Women shopkeepers abounded in colonial days, not only in New York, but throughout the northern colonies. They excited little comment, and received scant mention in the earlier sources. Apparently one Mrs. Goose, of Salem, sold groceries in 1643, for the court records of that year, giving probate of the will of Joanna Cummins, mentions that the latter owed Mrs. Goose for a pound of sugar.[1] Under date of April 4, 1690, Judge Sewall notes:[2]

This day Mrs. Averys shop, and Christian[3] Hefridge's shop, shut, by reason of the Goods in them Attached.

Not until well into the eighteenth century was advertising in the newspapers practiced to any extent, either by men or women. The first colonial paper, the "Boston Newsletter," was started in 1704, and the "American Mercury" (Philadelphia) and the "New York Journal" made their first appearance in 1719. Advertising by merchants

[1] *Quarterly Courts of Essex County*, vol. 1, p. 66 n.
[2] *Sewall Papers*, vol. 1, p. 317.
[3] Christian, used as a woman's name, is fairly frequent in colonial records.

amounted to little for some years, however, and women merchants appear to have hesitated longer than men about utilizing this kind of publicity. At first shopkeepers used the papers only to notify the public of a change of address or other unusual event. Widow Mary Copley apparently never bothered to advertise her tobacco shop until after she married Peter Pelham, the portrait painter. The "Boston Evening Post" for July 11, 1748, states:

Mrs. Mary Pelham, (formerly the widow Copley, on the Long Wharf, tobacconist,) is removed into Lindell's Row against the Quaker's Meeting House, near the upper end of King Street, Boston, where she continues to sell the best Virginia tobacco, Cut, Pigtail, and spun of all sorts, by Wholesale or Retail, at the cheapest Rates.

Many a shopkeeper, man and woman alike, is known only by the newspaper notices of death, or of settlement of estate. In 1739, the executor of Margaret Newman, of Philadelphia, widow, advertised that he would sell out her stock of "all sorts of mourning apparel, and sundry sorts of other goods at cheapest rates." [1]

The earliest regular newspaper advertisements were generally for one particular line of goods: in

[1] *Pennsylvania Gazette*, October 10, 1739.

1726 widow Gordon, of Philadelphia, was advertising tobacco, "London cut, at 2 shillings and sixpence the pound"; [1] in 1728 Mrs. Boydell, of Boston, had "choice green tea" for sale, [2] and Mrs. Stirling had "very good Bohea tea"; [3] in New York, in
1734 Mary Campbell was advertising Cheshire
cheese, [4] and the Widow Desbrosses, in Hanover
Square, "Oil of Olives, and Canary Wine at 6
shillings per Gallon by the five Gallons." [5] Either
the cost dropped or she was charging too much, for
next year [6] Ann Sleigh, in Duke Street, would sell
"very good Canary Wine at Five Shillings and
Sixpence the Gallon." In 1736 Widow Anna
Vanderspiegel resigned to her son her business of
selling window glass, by wholesale and retail. [7]

From the forties on, the advertisements became longer and more frequent. The following is
typical: [8]

Just imported in the last ship from London, and to
be sold by Hannah Cazneau in Water Street, Boston,
A great variety of women's Necklaces, Silk, Calli-
mancoe and Russel, Women's and Children's shoes,

[1] *American Mercury*, April 21, 1726.
[2] *Boston Newsletter*, August 1, 1728.
[3] *Ibid.*, September 19, 1728.
[4] *New York Journal*, May 20, 1734.
[5] *Ibid.*, October 28, 1734.   [6] *Ibid.*, January 12, 1735.
[7] *New York Journal*, February 21, 1736.
[8] *Boston Evening Post*, May 16, 1743.

Pattoons, and Clogs, also a variety of Ivory and Bone Stick Fans, the best of Pins and Needles, and fine Bohea and Green Tea.

The arrival of a ship was a particular incentive to advertise; frequently the name of the ship and the Captain are given, as: "Imported in the Hibernia, Capt. Child, from London, and to be sold by Mrs. Redmond, . . ." [1]

The idea of suiting the line of goods, or at least the advertisement of them, specifically to the time of year, made its appearance in the fifties; in the sixties, there were numerous women who advertised regularly, spring and fall.

A strict separation of kinds of goods evidently was not in vogue; the merchant with the most elaborate articles of dress was very likely to sell tea; and the grocer might slip in "women's and children's stays." Dry goods appear to have been the chief stock in trade of the greater number of our women merchants, however. One may suppose that the earliest stores specialized in useful articles such as were advertised by Bridget Treby, at her shop opposite the Golden Eagle, in Providence: [2]

. . . Irish linens; Sheetings; Holland; Dowles; Shalloons; Tammies; plain and spotted Lawns; fine and

---

[1] *Pennsylvania Gazette*, November 30, 1752.
[2] *Providence Gazette*, December 24, 1763.

22

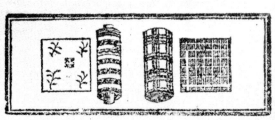

Imported in the last veffels from LONDON, LIVERPOOL, *and*
GLASGOW, *and to be fold, Wholefale and Retail, by*
MAGDALEN DEVINE,
*At her ftore in Second-ftreet, between Market and Chefnut-ftreets, and
nearly oppofite the Friends Meeting-Houfe, the following* GOODS,
*which (as fhe intends to decline the Retail bufinefs) will fell at
prime coft for* C A S H, *or on low terms for fhort credit, viz.*

COARSE, fine and fuperfine broadcloths, of various colours, 8-qrs. beaver coatings, red and blue duffils, plains and
kerfeys, 6-qrs. naps, of different colours and finenefs, fpotted
fwanfkins, plain and napt halfthicks, ftriped, worfted and cotton
linceys, red, white and fcarlet flannels, red and fcarlet ferges,
Mecklinburgs, half yard and half ell velvets and velverets, cam-
blets of various colours, ftriped and plain camblettees, fpotted
montees, yard wide ftarrets, fingle and double damafks, caliman-
coes, fhaloons, rattinets, durants, tammies, dorfetteens, poplins,
filverets, drefdenets, hairbines, hair grazets, taboreens and ruffels,
of different colours and finenefs, mens and womens yarn hofe,
mens and boys knit ribbed worfted ditto, mens, womens and boys
plain worfted ditto, mens and womens worfted ganze ditto, mens
filk and filk and worfted ditto, womens filk ditto, mens filk,
worfted and leather gloves, of various colours, womens filk,
worfted and leather gloves and mitts, Irifh and Ruffia brown and
white fheeting, 7-8ths and yard wide Irifh linens, Scotch and
German ozenbrigs, Ruffia and Irifh dowlas and diaper, Flanders
bed ticks, Englifh bed bunts and bed ticken, yard and 3-8ths,
yard wide, 7-8ths and 3-qrs. cotton and linen checks, 10 and 11
nail linen ditto, white and brown buckrams, check, linen, kent-
ing, black and coloured Irifh and Barcelona, filk and cotton romal
and bandanoe handkerchiefs, black filk neckcloths, 7-8ths and
yard wide cambricks and lawns, long lawns, humhums, book and
other muflins, ftriped, flowered and plain gauzes, catgut, fingle and
double purple, light, dark and pompadour ground chintzes, cotton
chintzes, cottons and calicoes, black and white blond laces,

A PART OF THE ADVERTISEMENT OF MAGDALEN DEVINE
Pennsylvania Gazette, November 24, 1768

THE SHE–MERCHANT

coarse Cambricks; Silk and Linen Handkerchiefs; Shirting and Apron Checks; cross barr'd Stuffs; Cambleteens; Women's Shoes and Goloshes, very neat; and Muffs and Tippits of the newest Fashions.

"Goloshes, very neat"! The styles have changed.

By the time we have actual evidence shops boasted an elaborate assortment of goods which would appeal to the most fastidious. One of the earliest long advertisements is as follows: [1]

TO BE SOLD

By Mrs. Benedicta Netmaker
At the Three Sugar Loaves and Cannister, in King Street,

Women's fine Silk, flower'd Russel, white Callimanco, Black Russel, black Shammy, and Girl's flower'd Russel Shoes, black Velvet, white Damask, and flower'd Silk Clogs, Women's Black and Children's Red Morocco Pumps, Women's Worsted and Thread Hose, Men's, Women's, and Children's Gloves, viz. Kid and Lamb, Coloured and black Glaiz'd, Black Shammy, and Women's white Cotton. Also super-fine Lawns, Cambricks, Cambrick Muslins, white Callico, Hollands, India Chints, Taffetys, Alamode, strip'd Lutestrings, fine Brussels lace, Silver, Padua-soy and other Plain Ribbons, Fans, Necklaces, Ear-ings, Masks, Wires and all other millinary and Haberdashery Wares.

Such fascinating lists continued to grace the pages

[1] *Boston Evening Post*, April 12, 1742.

23

of the sober press, and one may well imagine that the advertisers did a flourishing business. Apparently the ladies of Boston, despite their Puritan ancestry, were more given to the vanities of dress than those of New York or Philadelphia, but the Mrs. Redmond, before noted, tempted the Quaker dames of Philadelphia with mention of "Diamond rings, ear-rings, solitars, patch boxes," etc.

The vender of groceries has already been noticed, and it would seem that she made her appearance in force earlier than her sister who specialized in dry goods. If this be true, the explanation may be that clothing can be bought more conveniently in quantity, and that the early settlers who wished attire such as they could not make themselves were apt to write to friends in England, or to commission traveling neighbors to make purchases for them. Some imported articles of consumption, however, tea and wine in particular, were always in demand, not only by the rich, but by those who were unable to order direct from England, or in quantity. The assortment of groceries in stock gradually increased, and some of the later advertisements make it obvious that our forefathers did not need to mortify the flesh unduly. Take the following, for instance: [1]

[1] *Boston Evening Post*, March 9, 1772.

THE SHE-MERCHANT

TO BE SOLD CHEAP by
Mrs. Sheaffe,

At her Shop the North Corner of Queen street,
lately occupied by Mr. Joshua Green,
All Sorts of Groceries,
Among which are

Fresh Jar & Cask Raisins & Currants,

Superfine & Common Philadelphia Flour, by the barrell or smaller Quantity.

Rice-ground ditto,

Brown sugar by the barrell or Less

Choice Hyson tea at 20s per the single pound or less by the Quantity; also

Some of a superior Quality at 28s.

Bohea & Suchong ditto,

Coffee by the hundred or less

Very fine Chocolate by the box or Pound,

Spices, Citron, Almonds,

Capers Olives Anchovies

Race & Ground Ginger

Pepper Allspice Basket Salt

Cayanne Pepper

Very fine Mustard

Small Philadelphia Rusk by the Keg or Less

Split Peas in Bushel Casks, or by the Quart

Saltpetre,

Single refin'd Loaf Sugar by the Hundred or Loaf,

Also, a very excellent Sort of Double ditto in Small Loaves,

Florence Oil   Turkey Figs

Sugar Plumbs and Almonds

Tamarinds   Starch   Flax

Crown and Hard Soap

Hair Powder

Kippen's Snuff by the dozen or single bottle

Sago,   Barley   Velvet Corks

Oatmeal by the Bushel or smaller Quantity

15 & 18 Inch T D Pipes

Choice French Indigo

Brimstone   Allum   Copperas

Redwood   Logwood &c &c.

Also choice Frontineac Wine by the Case or Bottle.
Playing Cards, and an Assortment of Glass & China Ware.
**The above articles are the best of their kind, and she will esteem the Custom of her Friends and the Public as a peculiar kindness.

It is to be hoped that her friends and the public responded to this gentle request; at any rate, Mrs. Sheaffe continued to advertise until the Revolution

25

COLONIAL WOMEN OF AFFAIRS

put a stop to the newspapers of Boston. Her card
was sometimes short, a mere reminder that she
would still esteem custom "as a peculiar kindness,"
or again just a friendly notice that she had a new
and choice lot of "Frontineac Wine"; again, after a
while, an inventory like the above would be given.
Other women of colonial days advertised through a
longer period of years, but no one appeared in print
so many times in a year as she.

Temperance principles did not trouble the
women merchants of those days, nor were their
customers unduly restricted in choice. In 1766
Cornelia Blau, of New York, offered this interesting
assortment: [1]

Good Madeira, Lisbon, and Teneriffe Wines,
Cherry and Whortleberry Brandy, Anniseed, Orange
and Clove Cordials, Geneva, and Brandy, all by the
Barrel or Single Gallon.

Two lines of goods often associated with groceries
were seeds and china. A number of women in Boston advertised fresh importations of seeds every
spring; as they usually added, "and all sorts of groceries," one may suppose that they sold eatables between seasons on seeds. Their lists indicate the range
of vegetables on which our forefathers subsisted: [2]

[1] *New York Gazette*, August 28, 1766.
[2] *Boston Evening Post*, March 11, 1751.

THE SHE-MERCHANT

To be sold by Lydia Dyar
at the North End, near The Salutation,
The very best of Garden Seeds, early Cabbage, early
Lettuce Seeds, early Dutch, early Sugarloaf, early
Yorkshire, green Savoy, yellow ditto, large winter
Cabbage, Colliflower, early Dutch Turnip, round red
Turnip, yellow ditto, large Winter Turnip, three
sorts of Carrots, early Charlton Pease, early Hotspur
Pease, Marrow fat Pease, Dwarf Pease, all sorts of
other Seeds, Windsor Beans, Hotspur Beans, with a
variety of fine Flower Seeds, imported in the very last
Ship from London.

The trade in seeds must have been a profitable
one for women; ten have been noted who made a
specialty in it, and among these ten are some of the
most regular of colonial advertisers. For example,
Susannah Renken, who dealt in groceries, some
lines of dry goods, and china, advertised in the
Boston papers, every spring from 1764 to 1775 inclusive, a freshly imported stock of seeds. In the
same papers Bethiah Oliver made an annual announcement, from 1765 to 1771, inclusive; in 1772,
"Ebenezer Oliver informs the Publick and the Customers of his late Mother, Mrs. Bethiah Oliver,
deceased, that he sells at the shop formerly improved by her," and so on.

Dishes were naturally a favorite article, and
simple as they were in the days of the pioneers, the

variety had become bewildering before the Revolution. Imagine the joy, and the prices, could a modern collector look in at the following store: [1]

Elizabeth Perkins has for Sale at her shop, two doors below the British Coffee House in King-street, Boston,
A very large and Genteel Assortment of Cream colour'd Delph, Flint & Glass Ware, wholesale or retail, among which are cut, label'd, enamel'd, engrav'd & plain Quart, Pint, and ½ Pint Decanters, Cruits, Salts, Wine and Water Glasses, Tumblers, Jellies, Syllabub Glasses, Orange Glasses, Salvers, Sugar Dishes, Pattie, Sweetmeat and Pickle Saucers, Royal Arch Mason Glasses, Salt Linings, Water Glasses, Candle Sticks, etc.

Women tobacconists have already been mentioned. There were other lines in which at least scattering women's names are to be found. Several women dealt in furniture; the Widow Sharp, in Philadelphia announced her stock of

most sorts of Household Goods, as Bedsteds, Bedding, Chairs, Tables, Looking-Glasses, Pictures, Kitchin Furniture, etc. [2]

An enterprising merchant of Philadelphia was Hannah Breintnall, who kept shop at " the Sign of

[1] *Boston Evening Post*, July 12, 1773.
[2] *Pennsylvania Gazette*, July 13, 1738.

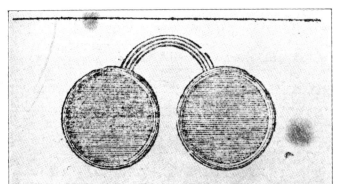

Juſt imported in the Snow Two Brothers, Capt. Marſden, from
London, and to be ſold by

HANNAH BREINTNALL,

At the Sign of the Speſtacles, in Second-ſtreet, near Black-
Horſe-Alley,

Variety of the fineſt Chryſtal Spectacles, ſet in Temple,
Steel, Leather or other Frames.   Likewiſe true Venetian
green Spectacles for weak or watery Eyes, of various Sorts. Alſo
Concave Spectacles for ſhort ſighted Perſons, Magnifying and
Reading Glaſſes, Teleſcopes, Perſpectives, with Multiplying
Glaſſes ; and Glaſſes for Davis's Quadrants, &c. &c. ⊕

"THE SIGN OF THE SPECTACLES"

Advertisement in the Pennsylvania Gazette, March 30, 1758

the Spectacles in Second-street, near Black-Horse-Alley," where she sold:

Variety of the finest Chrystal Spectacles, set in Temple, Steel, Leather or other Frames. Likewise true Venetian green Spectacles for weak or watery Eyes, of various Sorts. Also Concave Spectacles for short sighted Persons, Magnifying and Reading Glasses, Telescopes, Perspectives, with Multiplying Glasses; and Glasses for Davis's Quadrants, &c. &c. [1]

In a later advertisement, she mentioned " Ox-eye Glasses for taking Landskips," and added:

N.B. As the said Hannah Breintnall has settled a suitable Correspondence, she will constantly be supplied with the above Articles, which the Curious may at all times furnish themselves, in the completest manner at reasonable rates.

Unfortunately, the curious cannot satisfy themselves now as to what "ox-eye glasses for taking Landskips" may be.

Several drug stores were run by women, of which the following, inserted by the Widow Mankin in Market-Street, Philadelphia, is a sample: [2]

Lately arrived, a select Parcel from London, consisting chiefly of such things as are principally used in the Modern Practise of Physick, being a great variety

[1] *Pennsylvania Gazette*, March 30, 1758; May 16, 1765.
[2] *American Mercury*, November 21, 1734.

of Materia Medica, both simple and compound, Chymical and Gallenical.

Remedies, "Chymical and Gallenical," sound potent enough to cure anything.

Bookstores were sometimes kept by women. One of these was managed by Joanna Perry, the widow of Michael Perry, bookseller on King Street, Boston. Apparently she continued the business energetically, as several pamphlets are known to have been printed for her. She died in 1725.[1] Mrs. Elizabeth Bass advertised her bookstore in Philadelphia.[2] In 1773 Miss Ann Smith "returned to Philadelphia from a voyage to London, with a handsome assortment of books, and set up a bookstore." Unfortunately, she soon yielded to the importunity of an old sweetheart, who after marriage proceeded to manage his wife's business, and we are told that "the store then went to the dogs." [3]

Hardware, cutlery, and braziery were important articles of trade in the pre-Revolutionary days, and several women dealt chiefly in these. One of the most interesting of early shopkeepers is among them. Our first knowledge of Mary Jackson comes in 1744,[4] when "Robert Charles, in co-partnership

[1] Thomas, vol. II, p. 423.
[2] *American Mercury*, August 18, 1726.
[3] Thomas, vol. II, p. 449, and *Proc. A.A.S.* 1921, p. 102.
[4] *Boston Evening Post*, March 26, 1744.

with Mary Jackson," advertised that he was about to go to England, and desired all accounts to be settled before he went. Two years later, we read:[1]

All persons that have any Demands on the late Company of Jackson and Charles, are desired to bring in their accounts to Mrs. Mary Jackson, Administratrix, in order to a Settlement; and all those indebted to the said company are desired to pay their respective Dues, as they would avoid being sued.

There is nothing to indicate how long they had been in partnership or what their business was. The second question is presumably answered, however, in 1747, with the advertisement:[2]

Just imported, and to be sold by Mary Jackson at the Brazen Head in Cornhill, all sorts of Ironmongery, Braziery, Cutlery, also Pewter and Lead by the hundredweight, and Nails of all sorts by the Cask or smaller Quantity, at reasonable Rates.

Two months later,[3] she announced a new importation of mourning goods. In May, 1748, she had a handsome new chaise for sale; in September, lead, shot, and pewter dishes; in 1750, after the usual statement of imported goods, came this note:[4]

N.B. The said Mary makes and sells Tea-Kettles

[1] *Boston Evening Post*, October 6, 1746.
[2] *Ibid.*, September 28, 1747.
[3] *Ibid.*, November 23, 1747.   [4] *Ibid.*, June 11, 1750.

and Coffee-Pots, copper Drinking-Pots, brass and copper Sauce-Pans, Stew-pans, Baking-pans, Kettle-pots and Fish-Kettles &c.

The next year she added that she would sell "for cash or truck that will answer," and called attention to her new-fashioned tureens.[1] From 1753 on, she generally carried butter, sometimes Connecticut pork and Florence oil, but she always emphasized the hardware.

In February, 1759, the familiar card had an addition — "Mary Jackson and Son." In May, 1760, they informed their customers that they "have open'd their Shop, since the late fire, a few doors from the Town Hall." In 1761 they were back at the Brazen Head, selling braziery and butter as usual. But this was the last appearance of Mary Jackson's name, and in 1764 William Jackson alone at the Brazen Head was advertising cutlery goods.

The name Jackson is a common one, and it is impossible to identify her absolutely, but it seems probable that she was the Mary Goodwin who was married to William Jackson April 17, 1740; and the Mary Jackson whose will, naming her sons William and James, was probated December 8, 1780.[2]

[1] *Boston Evening Post*, June 3, 1751.
[2] *Probate Records*, Suffolk County, vol. 79, pp. 580–81.

THE SHE–MERCHANT

Another woman who carried on her husband's business with energy and success for many years, was Mrs. Sueton Grant, of Newport, Rhode Island. Her husband came from Scotland to this country in 1725, established an importing house, and married here. In 1744 he was killed by an explosion of gunpowder. His wife, who was left with several young children, immediately assumed the management of her husband's business, which included interest in several privateers, and relations with mercantile houses in England and on the Continent. When her son grew old enough, he assisted her, at first as a clerk under his mother's direction. Mrs. Grant was still carrying on an active and successful business at the time of the Revolution.

One incident may be quoted from "Reminiscences of Newport," which illustrates Mrs. Grant's force of character:

With large interests at stake, and having at times unscrupulous debtors to deal with, it is not surprising that occasionally she was drawn into litigation. In this instance at the last moment she discovered the duplicity of her counsel, and at once went to the court-room. Her lawyer, seeing her there, urged her to withdraw, but without effect; and when the judge, disturbed by the interruption, called for an explanation, she stepped forward, told why she was there, held forth the evidence of her counsel's treachery, and asked permission to argue her own case. The dignity of the woman, and her clear, business-like address to the court moved the judge, who allowed her to lay her case before the jury; this she did in a manner that left no doubt as to the truth of her statement, and the jury, after a short deliberation, gave her a verdict.

Much of the evidence regarding these women merchants is of so incidental a character that there seems reason for believing that a great many other women ran shops. The nature of the advertising makes it appear probable that any merchant who had a good-sized store after 1760 would advertise it; but in the earlier days, this would not follow at all. From 1740 to 1775, the names of about sixty women shopkeepers were counted in one paper alone — the "Boston Evening Post," Anything like continuous advertising, such as is common nowadays, did not come into vogue until near the end of that period; and many issues do not contain a business woman's name; but not a few others have nearly, and sometimes quite, half their advertisements inserted by women. Philadelphia has fewer women advertisers than Boston, and New York comes third. The difference is probably no greater among women than among the men, however, and may be accounted for by the difference in size of the cities, and perhaps partly by the greater popularity of advertising in Boston, owing to the longer time that newspapers had been established.

Some of the examples quoted show that women sometimes inherited their businesses; about as often they transmitted them to a son or daughter, or to another person. This was the case with Alice Quick, who sold dishes and dry goods at the "Sign of the Three Kings in Cornhill," and who advertised frequently from 1754 until 1761. In 1761 her executors gave notice of the settlement of her estate, and one of them, her nephew, Thomas Knight, announced that he would continue her business.[1] There is evidence that it was a business worth continuing; the account-book of Peter Faneuil shows that Mrs. Quick had imported through him goods to the amount of £1500 in one month.[2]

Partnerships were frequent. Mary Purcell and Jane Eustis started business together in 1755; apparently they did not agree, for in 1759 Jane Eustis was in business for herself, and in the same year Sarah Todd and Mary Purcell started a partnership which advertised extensively until 1773.[3]

[1] *Boston Evening Post*, November 23, 1761. (*Record of Boston Marriages*, 1700–1751, p. 134, gives the marriage of Alice Boucher and Richard Quick, May 12, 1726.)

[2] Earle, *Colonial Dames*, p. 56.

[3] *Boston Evening Post*, June 2, 1755; September 4, 1758; August 20, 1759 and ff.

COLONIAL WOMEN OF AFFAIRS

The words "for cash," or "for cash only," are frequently met with in the advertisements, but there is evidence that, whatever the preferences of the shopkeeper, she frequently allowed credit, and sometimes accepted goods in barter. Doris Viscount concluded a long notice in the "Boston Evening Post" for December 30, 1751 as follows:

The above articles to be sold in such quantities as will best suit the Buyers, for which I will take Pork or Beef in Payment, or other Commodity that will answer.

Those who allowed credit evidently had their troubles, and advertisements like the following are common: [1]

All persons indebted to Mrs. Hannah Lee of Marblehead, upon Bond, are desired to come and make speedy payment; and if not convenient to pay the money, to come and bring surety and change bonds into negotiable notes of hand, on Monday and Tuesday, the 22 and 23rd, and those neglecting will be sued in the December Court.

Not all the women shopkeepers proved successful. Mary Bennett had inserted short advertisements several times in the Boston papers of 1747; but in 1751 appears a notice regarding the estate of "Mary Bennett, spinster, deceased, represented insolvent." [2]

[1] *Essex County Gazette*, November 9, 1773.
[2] *Boston Evening Post*, September 30, 1751.

THE SHE-MERCHANT

During the black years of 1757–58, nowever, when Boston particularly suffered from the French and Indian wars, and notices of bankruptcy were in every paper, no woman was observed among the unfortunates. Women merchants shared, and took opposite sides in, the excitement regarding the Stamp Act. In the list of Salem merchants who protested against the Act the names of five women appear, and two are to be found among the four merchants who are advertised in the "Essex County Gazette" for November 13, 1770, for having imported goods contrary to agreement, and having "thus taken an ungenerous advantage of their fellow traders."

Anything like statistical accuracy as to the number of women who ran shops in colonial days is, from the nature of our information, impossible. The Census Bureau has published a study of "Women at Work" based on the census of 1900, which states that of the total number of persons who were merchants and dealers (except wholesale) 95.7 per cent were men, and only 4.3 per cent women.[1] (This, of course, does not include salespeople.) Any one who has read over a file of early newspapers will be convinced that the proportion of women was larger in colonial days. The names of

[1] *Women at Work*, Table XXII, p. 32.

all regular merchants advertising in the "Boston Evening Post" during the first six months of 1773 were counted, showing sixty-four men merchants, including eight partnerships, sex not known, but assumed to be men, as against six women, including one partnership known to be composed of women. These figures are too small to be worth much; but the resulting proportion of about nine and a half per cent appears to be a reasonable estimate.

CHAPTER III

THE ARTIFICER

THE treasured samplers, babies' bonnets, quilts and gowns, which grace the museums of our historical societies, show what exquisite handiwork the women of an earlier day could execute. Handiwork indeed it was, in the days when an electric sewing machine would have savored of the black arts; and gazing at the lovely pieces still extant, we feel sometimes as if our great-great-grandmothers must have been like the immortal Curly-Locks, whose one occupation was to "sew a fine seam."

Yet it may be admitted that these skillful ladies undoubtedly did wash the dishes, and eke feed the swine; at any rate, Bradford tells us, in 1623, "The women now wente willingly into the field, and tooke their little-ons with them to set corne." [1] Yet this, if not in, was emphatically for, the home, as Bradford is describing the difference in attitude which came about with the establishment of individual instead of communal holdings. Whatever the range of our grandmothers' activities,

[1] Bradford, p. 146.

from embroidering to planting, tradition holds firm
that all their work was for their own families alone;
unless, of course, in the way of charity.

Study of the available sources does not quite
confirm this view. As with the shopkeepers, so
with the producers it is difficult to find much
evidence before the establishment of newspapers;
but some hints may be discovered. For instance, the
New York tax lists for 1695 to 1699 give the
assessment of Mrs. Leisler's mill and ground, West
Ward, as 20 pounds, 3 shillings, 1 penny.

By the time we have much evidence on the
subject, the colonial lady was fully alive to the
value of charming attire, and her husband was
prepared to match her elegance with his own.
Many early diaries note the presence of itinerant
seamstresses; on one day Mrs. Holyoke, of Salem,
found time to write no more than "Mantua maker
here"; [1] and the Reverend Ebenezer Parkman
noted, "Miss Polly Howard here making lace for
my daughter." [2]

Some characteristics of dressmakers appear to be
perennial, as Nathaniel Ames found in 1758, when
he was an undergraduate of Harvard. He entered
his troubles in his diary: [3]

[1] *Holyoke Diaries*, p. 63.   [2] Parkman, p. 119.
[3] *Dedham Historical Register*, January 1890, p. 15.

Sept. 30, went to Molly Kingsberry to get her to make my Gowne, but now October 8th she hath disappointed me.

But young Ames was not to be trifled with, for the next entry reads:

Went to Boston got my Gowne.

The home-grown dressmaker had rivals, however, as the following indicates: [1]

Lately come from London, Mrs. E. Atkinson, who designs the making of Mantos and Riding dresses after the newest fashion, the taking in of all sorts of Millinary Work, teaching Young Ladies all sorts of Works, and dressing of Heads and cutting of Hair. Now living with Mrs. Edward Oakes's in Cornhill Street, Boston, near the Brick Meeting House.

The refinements of male attire were not forgotten, either, nor were children's needs overlooked. Thus in Philadelphia: [2]

Mary Cahell . . . makes and sells all sorts of gentlemens caps, Leather, &c. Also ladies and childrens caps, mantilets, pillareens, hoods, bonnets, long and short cloaks, mantles, and scarfs, with black bags and roses for gentlemens hair or wigs; all which she makes after the newest and neatest fashions, very cheap.

N.B. She makes turbans for Negroes.

[1] *Boston Newsletter*, March 27, 1729.
[2] *Pennsylvania Gazette*, March 4, 1746.

COLONIAL WOMEN OF AFFAIRS

"Black bags and roses for gentlemen's hair or wigs" sound almost unbelievably frivolous for the grave colonial fathers; and "turbans for Negroes" must have added a pleasant touch of color to the landscape.

In 1769 the alliterative "Mary Morcomb, Mantua Maker from London," was making negligées, Brunswick dresses, etc., as well as covering "umbrilloes," for the ladies of New York, "several of whom had declared their approbation of her work." [1]

The times of Watteau and Gainsborough saw the fan supreme in the colonies as well as in the Old World, and many women advertised mounting and repairing fans; Henrietta Maria East, in giving up her general shop, notified her patrons that she would "continue the fan business as formerly." [2]

Neither were the head-dresses less elaborate in this country, nor their proper adornment despised. In 1769, Anne Ducray, flower-maker from London, living in Pudding Lane, Boston,

begs leave to acquaint the Ladies that she makes and sells Head-Flowers, which for Beauty and color surpass those usually imported. Ladies may be supplied with single Buds for Trimming Stomachers,

[1] *New York Gazette*, July 10, 1769.
[2] *Boston Evening Post*, 1761.

PETIT-POINT OVERMANTEL PIECE DONE IN 1765 BY MISS DERBY, OF SALEM

The faces on the human figures are said to have been painted by John Singleton Copley. The piece has its original walnut and gilt frame. Length 4 feet, 2 inches

or sticking in the Hair. Good allowance made to Shopkeepers and Country Merchants who buy to sell again.

The beneficent function of Boston was already apparent, although displayed in disseminating buds for stomachers rather than sweetness and light of a more literary order.

The wicked thought occurs that possibly some of the grandmothers hired the making of those coveted samplers and caps; at any rate they might have done so, had they seen fit, as the following advertisement shows: [1]

Mrs. Mary Crabb, living near Fisher's Wharf, in the southerly Part of Boston, does all sorts of Drawing and Embroidering, with other Needlework, either in Gold or Silver, or plain, after the best manner; and she desires all Ladies and Gentlewomen who want any of the said Work done, to send it to her.

(The phrase "Ladies and Gentlewomen" occurs frequently in colonial newspapers, but what the distinction may be does not appear.)

It is hard to believe that any colonial dame shirked so obvious a duty as mending; but if such did exist she had ample opportunity to have the noxious work done for her. Elizabeth Boyd, in New York, announced: [2]

[1] *Boston Evening Post,* January 15, 1739.
[2] *New York Gazette,* October 10, 1748.

All sorts of stockings new grafted and run at the heel and new-footed; Also gloves, mittens, and Children's stockings made out of stockings; likewise plain work done.

Anne Scotton, of Philadelphia, ran a similar announcement in 1756,[1] to which she added: "mending Gentlemen's Knitt jackets and breeches." It is not surprising that her charms won the heart of one Mr. Jones, and in 1759, Anne Jones, formerly Anne Scotton, was still ready to do all kinds of mending.[2]

Fine laundering of laces, clear-starching (a special art in those days), and dyeing were favorite occupations. Starch was made by women also. For example, in 1737, Judith Brasher on Wall Street, New York,[3] "makes and sells stearch at 5d. per pound, or 4d. per pound by the hundredweight."

An enterprising woman was Sarah Brown, widow of Michael Brown, silk dyer from London, who in 1751 notified the Philadelphia public that she would continue her husband's business,[4]

where all persons may have all sorts of silks, quilted coats and gowns, silk stockings, gloves, and camlet clokes scower'd dy'd and dressed; burdets and tab-

[1] *Pennsylvania Gazette*, March 1, 1756.
[2] *Ibid.*, March 1, 1759.
[3] *New York Journal*, April 11, 1737.
[4] *Pennsylvania Gazette*, May 2, 1751.

THE ARTIFICER

bies water'd; men's clothes dry and wet scower'd, linnen and cotton dy'd blue, green, or yellow. Likewise mildew or stains taken out of pieces of silks or stuffs, or worsteds that are damaged at sea; all sorts of worsteds scower'd and pressed; all which works will be perform'd, in the most speedy, and after the most reasonable manner.

Presumably garments were "scower'd" for the same purpose as they are sponged now, in our less energetic days. Mrs. Brown continued to advertise off and on for the next ten years.

The following is by another courageous widow in Philadelphia: [1]

Mary Cannan, widow of Charles Cannan, late from Manchester, Taylor, deceased, . . . proposes to carry on the business of her late Husband with some sober qualified workmen they brought from England with them, and will esteem it a singular Favour if such, who were so kind to encourage her husband by their Employ in his first setting up in this City, would continue their custom, and will be obliged to any others to favour her with their Employ, as she hopes to be enabled to support herself and Family, and all Endeavors will be used to render her Employers Satisfaction.

N.B. She has some Cloths and Trimmings of sundry Kinds.

We hear much nowadays of the lazy housewife who serves her family with baker's bread and tri-

[1] *Pennsylvania Gazette*, December 22, 1763.

45

fles from the delicatessen store — such a contrast to her grandmother, who knew what went into everything her family ate. It appears as if some of these grandmothers must have been willing to entrust the making of their family's food to others, very much as is done now. The Philadelphia newspapers of 1741 and 1742 alone mention three different women who ran a bakery business. In 1752, Jane Bennet advertised that she would bake best pound cake, on order, one shilling a pound, material to be furnished by the purchaser.[1]

Advertisements of pickles and preserves were numerous, and appetizing reading they make. In the New York papers during the sixties and seventies, Widow Hetty Hays often tempted the public with such inducements as these:[2]

Cucumbers, peppers, peaches, Wallnuts, Mangoes, Beans, with several other sorts, all of which she puts up, either in pots or kegs, for shipping. She has also to dispose of, several sorts of country sweetmeats.

Apparently the fastidious Philadelphia taste could be gratified, as the following shows:[3]

Jane Moorland, from London, . . . begs Leave to inform the Public, that she prepares and sells Sausages, Black and White Puddings, Tripes and Cow-

[1] *Pennsylvania Gazette*, January 14, 1752.
[2] *New York Gazette*, August 26, 1771.
[3] *Pennsylvania Gazette*, December 31, 1761.

46

heels, likewise pickled Sheeps Tongues; which she sells ready boiled, or green, out of the Pickle. Whoever is pleased to favour her with their custom may depend on all the above Articles being done from the best Recepes, and in the nicest Manner.

In February, 1768, Mary Crathorne, widow of Jonathan, of Philadelphia, announced that she would carry on her late husband's business of manufacturing mustard and chocolate, and that upon notice she could fill any order, large or small, for export or otherwise; also that she would buy mustard seed in any quantity,

at those incomparible mustard and chocolate works at the Globe Hill on the Germantown Road, which her late husband was at a considerable expense in the erecting, and in purchasing out Benjamin Jackson's share.[1]

In October of the same year Benjamin Jackson and John Gibbons, using the same elaborate coat of arms and bottle which appeared over Mrs. Crathorne's name, stated that they had been unable to meet the demand for chocolate and mustard, "owing to the lack of seeds and bottles," but that they would be provided henceforth. Then follows this ungallant postscript: [2]

N.B. The said Benjamin Jackson is the Original,

[1] *Pennsylvania Gazette*, February 11, 1768.
[2] *Ibid.*, October 6, 1768.

and indeed only proper mustard manufacturer on this continent.

It would seem, however, as if the lady won, for we hear no more of Jackson and Gibbons, while Mrs. Crathorne was advertising the following year for an assistant.[1]

Another enterprising producer of foodstuffs appears in the following: [2]

Whereas Elizabeth Phillips of Philadelphia continues to cure and put up sturgeon in the best manner, different to any that has been put up in these parts, and given general satisfaction to those who have bought, either for exportation or for home consumption. The said Elizabeth Phillips is obliged to all persons who have hitherto favoured her with their Custom, and hopes the Fishery may meet with encouragement.
When you open the Keg, take out the cork and draw off the pickle in a clean pot or pan, take out the marked head, harden on the hoops, pour the pickle over the fish, putting a clean cloth upon that over the head, and the head of the keg upon that, with a small weight thereon, to prevent the air getting in; if the pickle waste, add sharp vinegar to it.

Then follows a list of shops where the sturgeon may be purchased.

The method sounds a trifle complicated; but the

---

[1] *Pennsylvania Gazette*, December 7, 1769.
[2] *Ibid.*, May 24, 1770.

MARY CRATHORNE,

Begs leave to inform the public (and particularly those that were her late husband's customers) that she has removed from the house she lately occupied in Lætitia Court, to the house lately occupied by Mrs. Aris, at the corner of the said court, in Market-street, where she continues to sell by wholesale and retail,

THE genuine FLOUR of MUSTARD, of different degrees of fineness; chocolate, well manufactured, and genuine raw and ground coffee, tea, race and ground ginger, whole and ground pepper, allspice, London fig blue, oat groats, oatmeal, barley, rice, corks; a fresh assortment of spices, domestic pickles, London loaf sugar, by the loaf or hundred weight, Muscovado sugars, choice raisins by the keg or less quantity, best thin shell almonds, olives and capers, with sundry other articles in the grocery way; likewise Madeira, Lisbon and Fyall wines in half pipes and quarter casks, and claret in bottles.

As the articles of mustard and chocolate are manufactured by her, at those incomparable mustard and chocolate works at the Globe mill, on Germantown road, which her late husband went to a considerable expence in the erecting, and purchasing out Benjamin Jackson's part; and as she has a large quantity of choice clean mustard seed by her, and the singular advantage of being constantly supplied with that article, she flatters herself, that upon timely notice, she can supply any person with large quantities of the said articles of mustard and chocolate, either for exportation, or for retailing again, when a good allowance will be made, and the same put up in any kind of package as may best suit the buyer.

N. B. All the mustard put up in bottles, has the above stamp pasted on the bottles, and also the paper round each pound of chocolate has the said stamp thereon; and least any person may be discouraged from bringing small quantities of mustard seed to her, from the singular advantages already mentioned, she therefore informs those persons, that may either have great or small quantities to dispose of, that she will always be ready to purchase of them, and give the highest price.

She also has two genteel eight day clocks, London make, with mahogany cases, which will be disposed of at a reasonable price.

ADVERTISEMENT OF MRS. MARY CRATHORNE
Pennsylvania Gazette, February 11, 1768

motive was similar to that so much in vogue now, of furnishing not an article but a service.

Good things to drink were as popular objects of women's endeavor in the moister days of the fathers as were good things to eat. Nor were these daughters of Hebe unappreciated by the sterner sex. The following letter in the handwriting of the President of Harvard College is to be found in the archives of the County Court of Middlesex for the year 1654: [1]

Honored Gentlemen, as far as it may stand in the wholesome orders and prudential laws of the country for the publick weal, I can very freely speak with and write in the behalf of sister Bradish, that shee might be encouraged and countenanced in her present calling for baking of bread and brewing and selling of penny bear without which shee canot continue to bake: In both which callings such is her art, way and skill, that shee doth vend such comfortable penniworths for the reliefe of all that send unto her as elsewhere they can seldom meet with. Shee was complained of unto me for harbouring students, unseasonably spending their time and parent's estate; but upon examination I found it a misinformation and that she most was desirous that I sh^d limit or absolutely prohibit any; that in case of sickness or want of comfortable bread or bear in the College only they sh^d thither resort and then not to spend above a penny a man nor above two shillings in a quarter of a year, which order she carefully observed in all or-

[1] *Cambridge*, p. 228.

dinary cases. How far she had publick allowance by the treasurer heretofore I leave to Brother Goff or any of our townsmen that are with you to shew; and how good effects for the promoting of the weal publick, and how Christian a thing in itself godly emulation is, as your historical knowledge informs you so your experience abundantly demonstrates, as contrariwise the undoing messures of monopolyes. The Lord to guide and prosper all your administrations shall bee the prayer of yours in which he can.

H. DUNSTER

The elders did not allow profiteering in those unamended days. In 1653, Dionis, the wife of Tristram Coffin, was "presented" in the September court for charging three pence a quart for her beer. She produced witnesses to prove that she put six bushels of malt into each hogshead, however, and as this was more than the law required, the court justly held that for a superior article she was entitled to charge a superior price, and she was discharged.[1] The record does not state whether the court was given an opportunity to sample the superior article. We may trust that Mrs. Coffin's business profited by the advertising.

More sophisticated sorts of liquids were produced by a later resident of Essex County. In the "Gazette" for April 14, 1772,[2]

[1] *Quarterly Courts of Essex County*, vol. 1, p. 303.
[2] *Essex County Gazette*, April 14, 1772.

THE ARTIFICER

Anna Jones informes the Public that she continues the distilling of Cinnamon, snakeroot, clovewater, aniseed, orange water, and many other sorts of spirits, all which she sells very cheap for cash, whole-sale or retail, at her shop opposite the Burying-Point Lane. The customers of her late husband, and all others who please to favour her with their Custom, may depend upon having the best of Spirits, and their Favours gratefully acknowledged.

Burying Point Lane, in Salem, ought certainly to harbor only the best of spirits, such as doubtless the customers of the late Mr. Jones found congenial.

Foodstuffs and clothing are, after all, quite within woman's accepted sphere, however unexpected fish-curing and men's tailoring may be. But there were not a few women who wandered much farther afield in making a livelihood: the Widow Gale, in Philadelphia,[1] and Sarah Goodwin, in Boston,[2] did chair-caning; Mrs. Goodwin advertised off and on from 1745 to 1756. Mary Emerson sold new and second-hand furniture, also silvered mirrors, and did joiner's work.[3] Ann Page, widow of John, turner, continued his business [4]

In all its branches, viz, for carpenters, joiners, chair-makers, &c, lignumvitae mortars and pestles, moulds

[1] *Pennsylvania Gazette*, December 5, 1754.
[2] *Boston Evening Post*, February 11, 1745.
[3] *Pennsylvania Gazette*, February 4, 1764.
[4] *Ibid.*, October 14, 1756.

for waggon, cart and chaise-boxes, and bench screws. Also iron turning for the West Indies, and mill spindles.

N.B. Spinning wheels are also made, mended, and sold at reasonable rates.

Several women were soap-makers and tallow-chandlers. One of these, Elizabeth Franklin, sister-in-law of Benjamin, carried on her business with energy, apparently in the face of trials. In 1756 she says: [1]

This is to notify the Publick, that there are sundry persons endeavoring to impose on them a sort of Soap which they call Crown Soap, a little resembling it in appearance, but vastly unlike in Quality, by which the character of the Soap has suffered greatly with People who have not taken particular notice, the Papers being so near the same as easily to decieve; and that there never was in New England any person but the late Mr. John Franklin that made the true sort of Crown Soap. It is now carried on by Mrs. Elizabeth Franklin at the Post Office, Boston, where they may depend upon being supplied with that which is good; and Hard Soap, Wax and Tallow Candles by wholesale and retail for Families or shipping.

Mrs. Franklin continued to advertise at frequent intervals, through the year 1766. In 1769 notice appeared of the settlement of her estate. [2] As her husband had been born in 1690, she was presumably well along in years.

[1] *Boston Evening Post*, November 8, 1756.
[2] *Ibid.*, January 23, 1769.

Other widows who carried on the business of their deceased husbands (businesses, one would think, not particularly suited to women) were Margaret Paschal, cutler,[1] Elizabeth Russell, coachmaker,[2] and Sarah Jewell, ropemaker, "at the same walk her late husband used on Society Hill, where all persons may be supplied with rigging and other work."[3] The women of Philadelphia excelled in the variety of their undertakings.

One of the oddest business inheritances, however, was that of Mary Salmon, of Boston, who

continues to carry on the business of horse-shoeing, as heretofore, where all gentlemen may have their Horses shod in the best Manner, as also all sorts of Blacksmith's Work done with Fidelity and Dispatch.[4]

(Mere *men*, one must suppose, could not expect a lady blacksmith to wait on them.) In a later advertisement Mrs. Salmon announced also her readiness to entertain boarders "in a genteel manner."

It is difficult to imagine that the genteel Mrs. Salmon herself fitted shoes to horses' feet. Some of these unexpected business women certainly did do the actual work themselves, however, as appears from the following:[5]

[1] *Pennsylvania Gazette*, May 23, 1754.
[2] *Ibid.*, August 29, 1754.   [3] *Ibid.*, March 21, 1748/9.
[4] *Boston Evening Post*, May 6, 1754.
[5] *Pennsylvania Gazette*, October 1, 1741.

These are to give notice that Mary Cowley on Society Hill does still continue with the assistance of her own Family to carry on the Business of Buckskin Dressing, she being of Ability to secure the Owners what they shall think fit to entrust her withall.

One is inclined to sympathize with a fellow craftsman of Mrs. Cowley's, who begins a notice of a clearance sale thus: "Rebecca Leech, declining to carry on the tanning business any longer." [1]

A different line of work is represented by Sarah Lancaster, "sive-weaver," who told her customers that she had removed from Market Street to Arch Street where she followed the said business, and bought good horse-hair in the usual manner.[2] Hannah Beales carried on her late father's business of net-making, and engaged "to supply any Person with seines, horse-nets, pigeon-nets, minny nets, casting nets, billiard table pockets, (!) and nets of every sort." [3]

In the previous chapter Mrs. Jackson, of Boston, has been mentioned, "the said Mary," who "makes and sells Tea-Kettles and Coffee-Pots, copper Drinking Pots, Brass and Copper Sauce-Pans, Stew-pans, Baking-pans, Kettle-pots, and Fish-

[1] *Pennsylvania Gazette*, December 26, 1752.
[2] *Ibid.*, May 3, 1739.
[3] *Ibid.*, March 12, 1767.

54

Kettles." A Philadelphia woman, Sarah Orr, also carried on a "braziery Business." [1]

Thompson's "History of Long Island" gives an account of an enterprising woman of the early days. This was Martha Turnstall Smith, who came to New York in 1683 with her husband, Colonel William Smith; they purchased large tracts on Long Island and erected St. George's Manor there. The husband died in 1705. In the first edition of his "History," Thompson states: [2] "the wife of Col. Smith is said to have been a remarkably intelligent and well-bred lady, and minutely skilled in domestic economy." In the second edition he amplifies this, with an interesting interpretation of "domestic economy": [3]

We present the following items from a memorandum in the writing of Mme. Smith, —

Jan. ye 16, 1707, my company killed a yearling whale, made 27 barrels.

Feb. ye 4, Indian Harry, with his boat, struck a stunt whale and could not kill it, — called my boat to help him. I had but a third, which was 4 barrels.

Feb. 22, my two boats, and my son's, and Floyd's boats, killed a yearling whale of which I had half, — made 36, my share 18 barrels.

Feb. 24, my company killed a small yearling, made 30 barrels.

---

[1] *Pennsylvania Gazette*, December 26, 1752.
[2] Thompson, p. 502.   [3] *Ibid.*, p. 348.

Mar. 17, my company killed two yearlings in one day; one made 27, the other 14 barrels.

Thompson gives the receipt for her tax, paid June 5, 1707, "£15, 15s., account of Mme. Smith, it being ye 20th part of her eyle." This indicates that she had taken in £315 worth of oil, not bad for a season's work.

Before the days of trusts and chain stores, businesses were smaller and were more often run by the proprietor himself, with only the aid of his his family. Occasional advertisements of "help wanted" show that outside assistance was sought, even in colonial times, and sometimes this was women's help. This study, however, is not considering women's work in subordinate positions, but its interest lies rather in cases where women were entrepreneurs — working with their own hands or hiring the hands of others; at any rate, working with their own brains. A good number of the businesses considered in this chapter were inherited. Undoubtedly less initiative is required to continue an existing business than to start fresh; yet it is but a short step from the recognition that women are competent to carry on almost any business to the admission that they are quite able to start out for themselves.

The occupations here considered demanded not

only business acumen, but in many cases considerable mechanical and executive ability. May it not be that the American shrewdness and inventive genius which have become proverbial are inherited partly from the distaff side?

CHAPTER IV

THE MINISTERING ANGEL

"O Woman! in our hours of ease,
Uncertain, coy, and hard to please,
And variable as the shade
By the light quivering aspen made;
When pain and anguish wring the brow,
A ministering angel thou!"

THIS qualified compliment has been paid to woman in all ages, and until recently it has been supposed that instinct would always teach her the right way to relieve pain and anguish, as surely as it guided Lady Clare in getting a drink of water for the dying Marmion.

Treatment as well as care of the sick, whether in the hands of men or of women, was largely a matter of inspiration in the first days of the colonies. Samuel Fuller, the doctor of Plymouth, had been a silk-maker in Leyden.[1] John Winthrop the younger, Governor of Connecticut, gave medical advice — not only in person, but also by letter, and purchased remedies for his friends when he was in London on diplomatic business.[2]

Women were not lacking among these avocational doctors. The obituary notice of Mrs. Mary

[1] Bradford, p. 39 n.
[2] *Mass. Hist. Col.*, 4th Ser., vol. VII, p. 492 ff.

Hazard, of Newport (grandmother of the Deputy Governor of Rhode Island), who died in 1739, in the one hundredth year of her age, states that "she was accounted a very useful gentlewoman, both to poor and rich, on many accounts, and particularly amongst sick persons for her skill and judgment, which she did gratis." [1]

It was not long, however, before this class was, if not supplanted, at least supplemented, by more trained physicians. One branch of medical practice alone was unaffected by the change — obstetrics. For over a century, midwifery was left to women; and in those days no woman had professional training. A Boston physician, writing in 1810, states: [2]

Obstetrical attendance, except in the most difficult cases, was seldom by male practitioners till within the last sixty years, but this part of the profession is now principally conducted by physicians.

Another doctor, writing ten years later, says that the employment of men accoucheurs was much more common in Boston than elsewhere. Arguing in favor of this practice, he goes on: [3]

It is obvious that we cannot instruct women as we do men in the science of medicine; we cannot carry

---

[1] *New York Gazette*, March 13, 1739.
[2] Bartlett, p. 13.   [3] *Boston Physician*, p. 7.

them into the dissecting room and the hospital; . . . and I venture to say, that a female could scarce pass through the course of education requisite to prepare her as she ought to be prepared, for the practise of midwifery, without destroying those moral qualities of character, which are essential to the office.

The doctor's disapproval of women in medicine was founded, after all, on a recognition of the need of training; and such disapproval was a necessary preliminary to proper training for women — a development which it is possible that this very physician may have lived to see.

Be this as it may, the midwife was an important member of colonial society; and indeed for a time had a legal monopoly of obstetrical work. In the town of Wells, Maine, in 1675, Captain Francis Rayns was "presented" in court "for presuming to act the part of a midwife," and was fined fifty shillings for the offense.[1] The famous Anne Hutchinson was a midwife before more spiritual cares engrossed her attention.[2] The records of the Essex County Court for March, 1657, granted administration on the estate of Isabell Babson, midwife inventoried at 27 pounds, 6 shillings, to her son James.[3]

The town of Rehoboth planned wisely in sending

[1] *Col. Maine Hist. Soc.*, vol. I, p. 380.
[2] Welde, p. 31.   [3] *Essex County Courts*, vol. II, p. 38.

for Dr. Samuel Fuller to become its physician, and at the same time to his mother, "to see if she be willing to come and dwell amongst us, to attend on the office of midwife, to answer the town's necessity, which at present is great." [1]

The church records of Dorchester, Massachusetts, give a glimpse of an industrious midwife: [2]

1705, Feb. 6th. Old widow Wiat died, having arrived at the great age of 94 years. She had assisted as midwife at the birth of upwards of one thousand and one hundred children.

Mrs. Wyatt's record was broken, however, by the wife of Thomas Whitmore, one of the pioneer settlers of Marlboro, Vermont, in 1763. Thompson, the historian of Vermont, says: [3]

Mrs. Whitmore was very useful to the settlers, both as a nurse and as a midwife. She possessed a vigorous constitution, and frequently travelled through the woods on snowshoes, from one part of the town to another, both by night and day, to relieve the distressed. She lived to the advanced age of 87 years, officiated as midwife at more than 2,000 births and never lost a patient.

Standards of training for nurses were even lower, if that be possible, than for midwives. Wet nurses, who hardly belong within the scope of this study,

[1] Bliss, p. 53.   [2] *Dorchester* (Boston, 1859), p. 281.
[3] Thompson, part III, p. 110.

advertised frequently as soon as newspapers were established. Ordinarily the printer acted as agent for them, and cards of both "nurse wanted" and "situation wanted" conclude with: "Enquire of the printer." The following shows that some characteristics of the nursing sisterhood have not changed radically: [1]

> Any person that wants a wet-nurse in a Family, may hear of one with a good Breast of Milk, that can be well recommended by the Printer. N.B. She is a married woman, but her Husband abroad; is a notable Housewife, and willing to put her hand to any sort of business. *A very rare Thing for a Nurse!*

The italics are the printer's.

Midwives did not advertise until quite late, and regular nurses, apparently, advertised not at all. Court records and tax lists name them, however, and they appear frequently in old diaries. Thus Jeremiah Bumstead writes under date of April 8, 1726: "Nurse Candige came to nurse my wife." [2]

One of the richest sources of information is the voluminous diary of Judge Sewall; he chronicles the many births, illnesses, and deaths of his own large family, and often of his neighbors', and usually mentions the officiating nurse, and midwife or doctor. He gives incidental glimpses of several

---

[1] *Boston Evening Post*, July 23, 1739.
[2] *New England Register*, July and October, 1861, p. 204.

curious customs. Thus, regarding the birth of his oldest child, he writes: [1]

April 1, 1677. . . . bad me call the Midwife, Goodwife Weeden, which I did. . . . Went home with the midwife about 2 o'clock (in the morning). Met with the watch at Mr. Rock's Brew house who bad us stand, enquired what we were. I told the Woman's occupation, so they bad God bless our labours, and let us pass.

April 8, 1677. Sabbath day, rainy and stormy in the morning, but in the afternoon fair and sunshiny, though a blustering wind. So Eliz. Weeden, the Midwife, brought the infant to the third Church when Sermon was about half done in the afternoon, Mr. Thacher preaching. After Sermon and Prayer, Mr. Thacher prayed for it. Then I named him John, and Mr. Thacher baptized him.

There are several entries concerning baptisms, where Midwife Weeden carried the baby; on December 13, 1685, he notes: [2]

Mr. Willard baptizeth my Son lately born, whom I named Henry. . . . Nurse Hill came in before the Psalm was sung, and yet the Child was fine and quiet.

This little Henry was not destined for many days on earth. [3]

Dec. 21, . . . Died in Nurse Hill's lap. Nurse Hill washed and layed him out.

[1] Sewall, vol. 1, p. 40.　　[2] *Ibid.*, p. 111.
[3] *Ibid.*, pp. 113-14.

Thursday, Dec. 24th, 1685. We followed little Henry to his Grave. . . . Midwife Weeden and Nurse Hill carried the corpse by turns.

Midwife Weeden officiated at the births of all except the youngest of the Sewalls' thirteen children; whether she had died, or moved away, does not appear. That she did a flourishing business seems probable, as Sewall several times mentions her being called away from his house to attend others.

A long list of nurses is named. The following entry regarding one has a very human ring: [1]

Jan. 13, 1701–2. I prayed earnestly by myself and in the family for a Nurse; Went and expostulated with Mr. Hill about his daughters failing me; in the mean time, one of his family went and call'd the Nurse, and I brought her home with me; which was beyond my expectation. For Mr. Jesse huff'd and ding'd, and said he would lock her up, and she should not come. I sent not for her, So I hope t'was an Answer of prayer.

This was shortly after the birth of his youngest child, when Hannah Greenleaf was midwife. A few days after the acquisition of Nurse Hill, he notes: [2]

My wife treated her Midwife and Women: Had a good dinner, Boil'd Pork, Beef, Fowls; very good Rost Beef, Turkey-Pye, Tarts. Madam Usher carved, Mrs. Hannah Greenleaf; Ellis, Cowell, Wheeler, Johnson, and her daughter Cole, Mrs. Hill our Nurse's

[1] Sewall, vol. II, p. 51.   [2] *Ibid.,* p. 51.

mother, Nurse Johnson, Hill, Hawkins, Mrs. Goose, Deming, Green, Smith, Hatch, Blin.

A grand occasion truly! Perhaps the Hill family knew what they were about when they saw to it that their daughter did not disappoint the Sewalls.

There were other advantages besides the prospect of a good meal, in being a nurse in attendance on a new baby. The following is but one out of many instances which might be quoted: [1]

July 28, 1714. According to my Promise, I carried my daughter Hannah to Meadford to visit Cousin Porter Lyeing in. Gave the Nurse 2s, Maid 1s. Hannah gave the Nurse 1s.

The nurses in the Sewall family received the reward of affection also. On December 9, 1713, the Judge notes his attending the funeral of Nurse Hannah Cowell [2] — "Was a very pious woman, and a true lover of the first ways of New England," and the following year he writes: [3]

August 7. Hearing of it just at the time, as I was with the Chief Justice, I went to the funeral of our excellent Nurse Hill.

The perquisites of a nurse had not diminished by 1772, when the little schoolgirl, Anna Green Winslow, wrote: [4]

[1] Sewall, vol. III, p. 11.   [2] *Ibid.*, vol. II, p. 410.
[3] *Ibid.*, vol. III, p. 14.   [4] Winslow, p. 15, and note, p. 100.

I made a setting up visit to Aunt Suky. It cost me a pistoreen to Nurse Eaton for tow cakes which I took care to eat before I paid for them.

The editor adds in a note:

There exists in New England a tradition of groaning cakes made and baked in honor of a mother and babe. These cakes which Anna bought of the nurse may have been groaning cakes. It was always customary at that time to give "vails" when visiting a new-born child; sometimes gifts of money, often trinkets and articles of clothing.

According to the Boston physician quoted above, the employment of men accoucheurs began to be common in the years following 1750. This may account for the fact that before that time no direct advertisements of midwives had appeared, but following 1760 several women address the public, always laying stress on their having "been examined by the Faculty," [1] or having "been approved by several gentlemen of that Profession." [2] The following card is the earliest of the kind noted: [3]

Mrs. Ridgely, Midwife, from London: Having practised for many years in that opulent city, with great success; but some affairs relative to the Death of her Husband making it indispensably necessary for her coming to this City, she intends during her stay to

[1] *New York Mercury*, July 4, 1768.
[2] *New York Gazette*, January 9, 1769.
[3] *Ibid.*, January 3, 1765.

resume that Practise, on a proper Recommendation, from Gentlemen of the Faculty; and will most carefully, tenderly, and punctually, attend those Ladies who may please to favour her with their Commands, on a firm dependance of exerting her Ability and utmost Endeavours, not only to merit their Esteem, but to prove herself on all Occasions, the Publick's very respectful and Obedient Servant,

SARAH RIDGELY

N.B. All letter or Messages to Mrs. Ridgely, at her House opposite William Smith's, jun. Esq., in the Broadway, will meet the due regard.

If it was true that the employment of men physicians for obstetrical cases was more common in Boston than anywhere else, there may have been a secondary reason for the removal to Salem noted in the following card.[1] This is interesting, as being the only instance found where a midwife specifically claims to have received instruction:

Mary Bass, midwife, from Boston, Beggs leave to inform the Ladies in this Place and the Vicinity, That having been instructed and recommended by the First Practioners in Midwifery in Boston; in compliance with the Request of Several Ladies, she has removed to Salem, where she intends to Pursue the Business of Midwifery. Any Lady, who may favour her with her Commands, may depend upon her earliest and best Attendance. Enquire at the House of Mr. Osgood, the corner of Prison Lane.

[1] *Essex County Gazette*, July 14, 1772.

COLONIAL WOMEN OF AFFAIRS

Perhaps the corner of Prison Lane did not prove an enjoyable location; at any rate, Mary Bass gave notice to her patrons the following year that she had moved opposite St. Peter's Church. She continued to advertise her readiness to serve until the Revolution put a stop to the newspaper.

Not only were our modern doctors and nurses foreshadowed in colonial times, but our too-familiar "benefactors of the race," who discover panaceas, have their early prototypes as well. The most advertised remedy in colonial newspapers (excepting only "Turlington's Balsam of Life") was "Mary Bannister's Drops of Spirit of Venice Treacle." In 1731, Edward Bannister announced in the Philadelphia paper that he could supply these drops;[1] it may be supposed that their originator had died before this date. Evidently this remedy received the compliment of imitation, for the "Boston Evening Post" in 1741 has a notice signed by Humphrey Wady, cautioning the public to beware of counterfeits, "there being no Person but myself and wife in New England that ever my Mother Bannister communicated the secret to."

Several women labored to preserve the health of the Pennsylvania public. In 1744, Ann Tatnall, of Darby, Chester County, announced that she

[1] *American Mercury*, July 1, 1731.

68

continued to make her "Powders" as formerly; [1] in 1748, Sarah Murray, of Philadelphia, gave notice that she prepared and sold "Tar Water," from the best tar.[2] The first of many similar advertisements appeared in September, 1751, as follows: [3]

Catherine Deimer, at the upper end of German-town, at the house of Isaac Will, hereby gives notice, that those that are afflicted with scald heads, and will apply to her, may find immediate relief. If she does not cure it effectually, she asks no money. Those inclined to make use of her, are desired to do so before the weather grows cold, because there is a greater difficulty and expense in the cure in cold than in warm weather.

Apparently she prospered, for in 1754 she gave her address "At the sign of the Comb," and went on, "having for many years past had the practise of curing that most raging distemper commonly called The Scald Head," etc.[4] Two years later she announced that she would sell the salve, for the benefit of those living at a distance.[5] Mrs. Deimer seems to have died in 1761 or 1762, for in July, 1762, John and Elizabeth Bellin, also at the "Sign of the Comb," have a long announcement that

[1] *Pennsylvania Gazette*, February 17, 1744.
[2] *Ibid.*, August 4, 1748.   [3] *Ibid.*, September 5, 1751.
[4] *Ibid.*, July 4, 1754.   [5] *Ibid.*, May 20, 1756.

they will sell "Catherine Deimer's Ointment," and "Deimer's Pills for the Gravel and Pain in the Back"; and that they will take persons into their homes for treatment.[1] They continued to advertise until 1771.

Apparently "scald head" was a familiar demon in colonial times, for in the year that Catherine Deimer made her first appearance Hannah Pearson, of Philadelphia, concluded an advertisement regarding real estate thus:[2] "N.B. The said Hannah Pearson can cure a scal'd head."

Certain preoccupations of the fair sex seem to have been very much the same in early days, even in the staid Quaker City, as they are now, if the following may be taken as evidence:[3]

To be sold by Nurse Tucker, living next Door Below the Sign of Lord Loudon, in Front Street, an extraordinary Ointment for Clearing the Skin, taking off Freckles, and all kinds of Roughness, is good to soften the skin, and many other Things beside, too tedious to mention; also a Tooth Powder for whitening the Teeth, and Preserving them from the Scurvy; likewise silk Pomatum. Any Person by applying to the said Tucker the first Time they have the Toothache, shall be perfectly cured.

It may be, however, that this was too frivolous for

[1] *Pennsylvania Gazette*, July 1, 1762.
[2] *Ibid.*, March 5, 1751.   [3] *Ibid.*, May 27, 1762.

her patrons, for in 1765, when announcing a change of address, she called attention to

the following articles, viz: A choice ointment for curing the Piles, Rheumatism, strains, all kinds of Pains, Ring-worm, Moths, Carbuncles, Sun-burning, Freckles, and chopping of the Skin; and Women that are likely to have sore Breasts, if they apply in Time, it will certainly be of great Service to them. Likewise a Powder for curing the Toothache, and keeping the Scurvy from the Gums. And Pills for cleansing the Blood, and a gentle Purge. Any Persons that have old Sores to cure, may apply to the said,

ANN TUCKER [1]

This sounds serious enough to satisfy any one.

The ladies of New York also had an opportunity to indulge their vanity. As early as 1736 we read: [2]

To be Sold at Mrs. Edwards, next door to Mr. Jamison, opposite the Fort Garden, an admirable Beautifying Wash, for Hands, Face, and Neck, it makes the Skin soft, smooth and plump, it likewise takes away Redness, Freckles, Sun-burnings, or Pimples, and cures Postules, Itchings, Ring-Worms, Tetters, Scurf, Morphew, and other like Deformities of the Face and Skin, (Intirely free from any Corroding Qualities) and brings to an exquisite Beauty, with Lip Salve, and Tooth Powder, all sold very Cheap.

If the poor women of New York suffered from

[1] *Pennsylvania Gazette*, February 21, 1765.
[2] *New York Journal*, March 29, 1736.

these and "other like Deformities," one must hope
that they patronized Mrs. Edwards generously.

Other annoying afflictions besides the scald head
apparently moved in better society in the days of
our forefathers, than among their squeamish descendants. The "Boston Evening Post" for March
28, 1748, contains this interesting announcement:

Hannah Chapman makes and sells a Smell in Mixture, that will cure the Itch or any other breaking
out, by the Smell of it. Enquire for me at the Sign
of the Stayes at the Head of Seven-Star Lane.

Cupid works under strange circumstances, and
perhaps he touched the heart of a grateful patient,
for the Boston marriage records give the marriage
of Hannah Chapman and Matthew Kitchin on
June 26, 1751.[1] Cupid, however, did not interfere
with Hygeia, as on February 28, 1758, we read:

Hannah Kitchin makes and sells a smelling Nectar
that will cure the Itch, or any other breaking out only
by the Smell.

Apparently there was competition for the post of
most successful healer of the itch, and one wonders
if Mrs. Kitchin was among those slightingly referred to in the following: [2]

[1] *Boston Marriages*, 1700–05, p. 297.
[2] *Boston Evening Post*, May 3, 1762.

THE MINISTERING ANGEL

Agnis Gordon, the Daughter of Dr. John Tucker, living in Mrs. Harrod's house, the Baker, makes a mixture that will cure the Itch or any other Breaking out. There be many that pretend to make it, who know nothing about it, near Charleston Ferry.

Generally we can get only the merest glimpse of these women, but a somewhat fuller portrait can be reconstructed of one woman — Lydia Darragh, of Philadelphia.

Mrs. Darragh's first appearance, in the "Pennsylvania Gazette" for December 4, 1766, is unique:

The subscriber, living in Second Street, at the corner of Taylor's Alley, opposite the Golden Fleece Tavern, takes this method of informing the Public that she intends to make Grave-Clothes, and lay out the Dead, in the Neatest Manner, and as she is informed a Person in this Business is much wanted in this City, she hopes, by her Care, to give Satisfaction to those who will be pleased to favour her with their Orders.

LYDIA DARRAGH

Subsequent information indicates that she found more scope for her labors in assisting people into rather than out of the world; one hopes that she did not attempt to combine the occupations. Apparently she was versatile, for the genial German diarist of Philadelphia, Jacob Hiltzheimer states:

73

October 15, 1774 ... I was suddenly seized with a great pain in my right hip and forced to return. Doctors Cadwallder, Bond, and Kearsley were immediately summoned to my bedside, but could give but little relief.

Oct. 17. My pain still continued excessive, but with the help of a clever little Irish woman named Darrah, I got some relief by a clyster.

Mrs. Ellet, in "American Women of the Revolution," published in 1849, pictures Mrs. Darragh from a different angle. She says: [1]

This anecdote is given in the first number of the "American Quarterly Review," and is said to be taken from Lydia's own narrative. It is mentioned or alluded to by several other authorities and in letters written at the time. The story is familiar to many persons in Philadelphia, who heard it from their parents; so that there seems no reason to doubt its authenticity.

The story, in brief, is as follows:

During the British occupation of Philadelphia, the British officers sometimes held their meetings in the house of William and Lydia Darragh, members of the Society of Friends, who lived on Second Street, directly opposite General Howe's quarters. (These were probably in the Golden Fleece Tavern, noted in Mrs. Darragh's advertisement.) The Darraghs' house may have been

---

[1] Ellet, vol. 1, p. 171 and ff.

chosen because of the peaceful proclivities of its inhabitants. On December 2, 1777, an officer went to Mrs. Darragh, and gave orders that her room should be prepared for that evening, and laid special stress on his wishing the family to go to bed early, in order that the meeting might be undisturbed; he said that when it was over, he would knock on her door, so that she might let them out and lock up. Lydia obeyed these orders, as far as her family were concerned, and after admitting the officers she went to her own room, but — alarmed by the unusual precautions — she did not undress. After long and painful hesitation, she stole to the door of the room where the meeting was being held, and listened long enough to hear an order read for the troops to leave the city on the night of the 4th, and attack the Americans at White Marsh. Then she went to bed, but — we may be sure — not to sleep. When the meeting was over, the officer knocked; she did not answer him, however, until he knocked several times. Next day she said nothing, even to her husband, except that the family needed flour. Starting early, without difficulty she got a permit from General Howe to pass the British lines, as she had often asked for one before when going for flour. She then walked four or five miles to the mill at Frankford, where she left her bag; she pressed on toward the American camp, but on the way fortunately met an American officer, whom she knew by sight, and to whom she told her news. Then she went back for her bag of flour, and walked home again. After the failure of the British attack, the same British officer came to see her, and asked if any of her family were up on the night of the meeting. One may imagine how her heart beat, but she answered truthfully, "No, they all went to bed at eight o'clock." "It is strange," he replied; "you, I know, were asleep, for I had to knock three times before you heard me." No more was said, and the little Quakeress was thankful to have escaped the need of a verbal lie — or perhaps worse.

Mrs. Darragh died on December 29, 1789. The next number of the "Pennsylvania Mercury" contained this obituary.[1]

On Tuesday evening last, died Mrs. Lydia Darragh, and on Thursday her remains were interred in the Friends' burial ground attended by a numerous concourse of sorrowful citizens.

She had experienced some share of those ills attendant on humanity, and applied herself, for the support of her family, to a profession, in which the female part of society experienced her skill, tenderness, and assiduity, — to all she extended her sympathy; the poor and unfortunate will long, and the wealthy do now, lament the loss of it. She found

[1] *Pennsylvania Mercury*, January 2, 1790.

the rewards of decent competency, of universal respect, and "the blessings of many ready to perish." Let her example enliven the hope of the industrious, and give strength to the virtuous; trusting as she always did in her severest afflictions, that a good Providence will in due time, bless the labours of the compassionate and tenderhearted.

The style and the sentiment of this obituary strongly suggest the pen of the aged Franklin, who was still writing at this date. Whoever the author, however, it is worth much to have lived and worked so as to leave such a reputation.

CHAPTER V

THE SCHOOL DAME

THE idler in the old cemetery at Cambridge, just across from Harvard University, may still read this tribute to Mrs. Murray, who died in 1707, at the age of sixty-two:

> "This good school dame
> No longer school must keep,
> Which gives us cause
> For children's sake to weep."

The school-teacher has always been a respected member of society in this country, and Mrs. Murray was one of a host, little known to fame, but honored in their day.

Both the English and the Dutch brought with them to the New World advanced ideas about popular education, and scarcely had they built their houses when they began to plan for schools. The first school in New Amsterdam (now New York City) was started in 1633.[1] Boston had a school in 1635.[2] The earliest colonial law requiring the establishment of schools, passed in Massachu-

---

[1] Randall, p. 3.
[2] *Memorial History of Boston*, vol. IV, p. 237.

setts in 1647,[1] decreed that every town of fifty families should maintain a common school, and every town of one hundred families, a Latin school; the expenses for these schools might be raised either directly from the parents of the children who attended or from the town at large. As the former method seems to have been in considerable favor, it is not always possible to trace the existence of the school through the town records, as was the case where the teacher's salary was voted by the town fathers. A study of the early records, however, shows that by 1670 or 1680 the common schools were frequently taught by women. It should be borne in mind that in early days women by no means had a monopoly even in the lower grades; it is not certain that they had a majority. The Latin schools, which were in essence college preparatory schools, were taught exclusively by men for many years.

The fathers seem at first to have given about the same reward to women as to men for teaching these primary schools. The reward, however, was not such as to arouse envy in the heart of any over-worked and underpaid teacher of to-day. The town records of Woburn, Massachusetts, state that the selectmen appointed Widow Walker "to be a

[1] *Mass. Colonial Records*, vol. II, p. 203.

school dame for the year 1686, and to have tenn shillings for her labour, as the other [mistresses before her] had." [1] And Mrs. Walker furnished the schoolhouse too! The records of Woburn and of other towns confirm the implication that this was a common rate of pay. [2]

The price rose in time, however. In 1715, the town of Lexington appropriated fifteen pounds for the support of a school through the year, taught by a man. In the following year, this was modified as follows: [3]

May 14, 1716, — *Voted* that all scollers that com to school, to pai two pens per week: for Reeding, and : 3 : pens for righting and siphering and what that amounts to at the years End: so much of the fifteen pounds to be deducted and stopt in the Town Treasury whilst the next year.

In 1717, it was felt that a single school was not sufficiently convenient for the younger children, and that other schools were needed in different parts of the township. The record for July 21 states that it was voted:

y[t] Clark Laurances wife and Epheram Winships wife keep Schools; from ye day of ye Date hereof; until ye last day of October next following; and if

[1] *Town Records of Woburn, Mass.*, vol. III, p. 93.
[2] For a fuller discussion, see Small, pp. 164 ff.
[3] *Lexington*, pp. 379 ff.

they have not Scholers sufficient as to number; to amount to 5 shillings per week; at 3 pence per Scholer per week; Dureing ye Terme above Sd; Then ye Town to make up what Shall be wanting of ye 5 Shillings per week.

One hopes that the "3 pence per Scholer per week" indicates that a study of "Righting and Siphering" was no longer optional; a study of spelling doubtless appeared unnecessary.

The records of nearly every town bear the names of some school-mistresses. A careful study of the records of Dedham, Massachusetts, to learn as much as possible regarding the early schools, whether taught by men or women, has been made by Carlos Slafter, in the "Dedham Historical Review," beginning July, 1890. Women, evidently, made their appearance in the teaching profession much later in Dedham than in many towns, for the earliest whom Mr. Slafter finds was Mary Green, who taught the summer session of 1757. It was not the custom in those days to waste valuable time in long summer vacations; and women were favored in many places for teaching the summer term while men were busy on the farms. In Dedham, where there were several different schools, so that distances should not be too great for the younger children, eight different women figure as teachers of the summer sessions, for the years 1757, 1758, and 1759. Some of these women taught in subsequent years also. In 1760, the winter session was first entrusted to a woman, Mehetabel Ellis. Thereafter, women frequently taught the entire year. Nineteen different women are named as teachers between 1757 and 1775.

One of these women evidently had ideas about the place of woman in the teaching profession. Susannah Brittano, who taught the summer session for four years, died in 1764, leaving all her personal estate, valued at about $100, to establish a school in the Third Parish of Dedham to be taught by a woman.[1] The historian of the Third Parish of Dedham names fifteen teachers who were paid out of this fund, before rising prices made a rearrangement necessary. But one can feel quite sure that the object of Miss Brittano's bequest has been attained; and that a woman still teaches school in the Third Parish.

Sources of information about schools are more abundant and available regarding the towns in New England than regarding the South, but women did their part there also. The author of "Notable Southern Families"[2] records the achievements of Kate Brownlow, who with her husband James

---

[1] Slafter, p. 113 ff.   [2] Armstrong, vol. I, p. 39.

emigrated to America about the year 1745, coming from County Antrim, Ireland. For several years both taught school in Lexington, Rockbridge County, Virginia — James teaching the boys and Kate the girls. They then moved to Abingdon, in southwestern Virginia, where they followed the same procedure. Mrs. Brownlow has another achievement to her credit besides that of teaching school. She was the mother of one daughter and six sons, from whom, it is said, every one in the United States of the name of Brownlow is descended.

The reader has already made the acquaintance of Madam Sarah Knight, through the trenchant descriptions she gave of some early inns. Madam Knight obtained her title of "Madam," by which she is usually called, because of her experience as a school-mistress. She was born in Boston, in 1666, the daughter of Captain Thomas Kemble. Her husband, Richard Knight, of Boston, died in England probably not long before 1704, the date of her famous journey. After her return, she opened a school in Boston — Benjamin Franklin and Samuel Mather being the most celebrated of her pupils. In 1714, she sold her house in Boston and moved to Connecticut, where her only child, Mrs. John Livingston, lived. Madam Knight purchased land

extensively around New London. She kept house in
Norwich, but spent much of her time on her farms
in New London, at one of which she maintained a
tavern.[1]

Regarding Madam Knight's accomplishments as
a teacher, the daughter of Samuel Mather, Mrs.
Hannah Mather Crocker, wrote in 1818: [2]

Among some of the early instructors of writing may
be found Mrs. Sarah Knights, in the year 1706. She
was famous in her day for teaching to write. Most of
the letters on business and notes of hand, and letters
on friendship were wrote by her. She was a smart,
witty, sensible woman, and had considerable influence
at that period.

A perusal of the Journal inclines one to accept this
characterization; and one cannot but wish that a
woman who was witty and sensible, and who wrote
the important letters for her community, had found
time to write further letters for posterity. What
entertaining "Mirrors of Boston" might she not
have indited!

Judge Sewall names several school-mistresses of
Boston in his diary, and shows the affectionate
respect with which they were regarded by their
neighbors. The earliest notice is under date of
January 7, 1686/7.[3]

[1] Knight, Introduction. [2] Crocker, p. 66.
[3] *Sewall Papers*, vol. I, p. 164.

THE SCHOOL DAME

This day Dame Walker is taken so ill that she sends home my Daughters, not being able to teach them.

The daughters must have been Hannah, then seven years old, and Betty, aged five.

In May of the same year, Sewall records the death of Dame Walker's husband, Robert Walker. In December, 1695, he tells of the illness and death of Dame Walker herself.[1]

Dec. 19. I was with Dame Walker, and Sam. came to call me; I told her Sam. was there; she prayed God to bless him and all my posterity.
Seventh Day, Dec. 21. Between 8 and 9, I went to see Dame Walker and found her very weak and much altered. . . . But before I could get away, a Girl came runing to call me. And by the time I could get thither, the Good woman had expired.

Sewall is in the habit of naming the bearers at the funerals he attended, and few included names of more of the leading people of Boston than did that of Dame Walker, December 23, 1695. After describing the funeral he adds: [2]

Note. After Sam. came home, he was exceedingly affected, shed many tears, and is even overwhelmed with Sorrow: the Lord grant that the removal of one of his best friends may put him upon seeking unto God betimes and making Him his Hiding Place.

Sam, the Judge's eldest son, was then seventeen

[1] *Sewall Papers*, vol. I, p. 416 ff.   [2] *Ibid.*, p. 418.

years old. He was a rather difficult youth to handle, and proved a problem to his parents for a good many years. His grief for his old teacher is perhaps a truer witness to her good qualities than all the encomiums of the charitable Judge.

A subsequent entry comes as rather a shock to the present-day reader, accustomed to the use of telegraph and express train in times of family trouble: [1]

Jan. 11, 1695/6. I wrote a letter to Mr. Zech. Walker, acquainting him with his Mother's death and Funeral. — I delivered this letter to the Post on Second day morning, Jan. 13, 1695/6.

(Zechariah Walker was the minister of Stratford, Connecticut.)

Some of the Sewall children attended other dame schools besides that of Mrs. Walker, who perhaps had retired by 1691, when the Judge notes: [2]

April 27. This afternoon had Joseph to school to Capt. Townsend's Mother's, his Cousin Jane accompanied him, carried his Horn-book.

It seems scarcely possible that the date of this entry can be correct, as Joseph, the diarist's second son, was born August 15, 1688, and hence would be less than three years old at this time; but Judge Sewall

THE SCHOOL DAME

is ordinarily accurate. As this little twig was bent, so the tree inclined, for Joseph became a distinguished clergyman, pastor of the Old South Church, and was even elected President of Harvard College, although from modesty he declined the honor.

Captain Townsend's mother was not the only woman who helped to educate Joseph, for in 1695, when he had attained the great age of seven, his father wrote: [1]

Aug. 27. — In the morn I had Joseph to Mrs. Kay's to School at Mr. Trott's house.

Perhaps it was not considered necessary to begin a girl's education quite as young as a boy's, but the girls in Judge Sewall's family were not seriously neglected. Mary, born October 28, 1691, began her schooling thus: [2]

2nd day, Nov. 2. (1696). Mary goes to Mrs. Thair's to learn to Read and Knit.

During the epidemic of smallpox in 1721, Sewall noted: [3]

*Octob*ʳ 16. Mrs. Martha Cotes, Mistress of our Charity-School, was buried; . . . Had a great Character as to devotion and piety.

It is highly probable that nothing correspond-

[1] *Sewall Papers*, vol. I, p. 411.   [2] *Ibid.*, p. 436.
[3] *Ibid.*, vol. III, p. 293.

87

ing to the modern conception of a private school existed for a generation or more, at least, after the settlement. By the time that newspapers were becoming common, however, it is evident that genuine private schools had been established in the larger towns. The teachers of the local "dames schools," to which boys and girls went together to learn to read, probably felt themselves too much a matter of course in the community to need to advertise; at any rate, one learns little about them from the press; on the other hand, notices of more advanced schools, and schools which taught special subjects, are abundant. The following is an early example, taken from the "American Mercury" (Philadelphia) of May 16, 1723:

Publick Notice is hereby given That there is lately arrived in this city one Mrs. Rodes who will teach any young ladies or Gentlewomen to read and write French to perfection. She will give constant Attendance at her Dwelling-House in the Second Street in the Alley next door to Dr. Owens. She likewise teaches to flourish on Muslin after the most expeditious way, and at very reasonable Prices. She likewise draws all Manner of Patterns for Flourishing on Muslin, and those in Fashion of Lace, which is very pretty and quickly learned. She likewise draws Patterns for Embroidering and Petticoats, etc. And those who have a Mind to learn, she will teach very reasonable. She hath very good Orange-Oyl to dispose of by the Quarter of a Pound or Ounce; the said Oyl being very good for the Wind-Cholick and Stomach, and fit for many other Things. And likewise Sweet-Meats, as Lemon and Orange-Peel, very well made; it will be disposed by the Pound, Half-Pound, or Quarter, very cheap.

N.B. She gives attendance from Nine in the Morning till Twelve, and in the Afternoon, if any Gentlewomen require it, at their Houses. As she is but a New-Comer to this Place, all persons, who have a mind to know more, may inquire at Mrs. Rachel Renier in Chestnut-street, and she will inform them.

This serviceable blue-stocking surely deserved success; but one suspects that the number of "ladies and gentlewomen" who wish to learn French, even to "speak and write French to perfection," was, alas, but small.

Mr. and Mrs. John Dommet taught school, also, in Philadelphia, on much the same plan as that followed later by the Brownlows in Virginia; John Dommet required ten lines in the "American Mercury" of March 19, 1730, to enumerate the different subjects which he was prepared to teach to young gentlemen at reasonable rates; then he adds this succinct postscript:

N.B. His Wife also Teaches Reading, Knitting, and all Sorts of Needle Work, very cheap.

Boarding-schools were making their appearance

at this period, and Boston early became a favorite location. In the "Boston Gazette" of May 24, 1736, one reads:

This is to give Notice that Mrs. Sarah Todd has now opened a school to teach young Women Writing, and Cyphering, at the House of Mrs. Anne Dowding, in Corn Court near the Dock Market, Boston; also will wait on Gentlemen's Children at their House if desired, between School Hours.

At the same House young Gentlewomen are Boarded and all sorts of Needle Work is taught.

It is charitable, and probably reasonable, to assume that the young gentlewomen who benefited from these boarding or day schools, had already learned to read and write, and possibly to "Cypher" a little. At any rate, out of thirteen schools advertising in the "Boston Evening Post," this of Mrs. Todd's is the only one which mentions instruction in any subject which could be classified as academic. Out of eight teachers noted in the Philadelphia papers, two besides Mrs. Dommet spoke of reading or writing, although one of these appeared doubtful of the demand: [1]

Mrs. Jane Voyer proposes to open a school in this city, to teach young Ladies French and Writing, if suitable encouragement appear within two weeks of this date. A subscription paper for that purpose con-

[1] *Pennsylvania Gazette*, March 11, 1749.

taining the conditions &c, may be seen at the Post-office.

The teaching of French was more popular in Philadelphia than elsewhere. Mrs. Voyer and Mrs. Rodes have been quoted already, and Margaret Hair described herself as proficient in the French language,[1] but it is quite possible that, like Chaucer's Prioress, she spoke:

> "After the school of Stratford atte Bowe,
> For French of Paris was to her unknowe."

Of the five schools noted in the New York papers, two gave instruction in reading. The earlier of these would hardly appeal to the mothers of young ladies to-day, as it was held "in the House at the Back part of Mr. Benson's Brew-House."[2] The other school referred to, however, leaves nothing to be desired by the most fastidious:[3]

SARAH HAY

Takes this method to inform the public that she proposes to open a Boarding School, the first of May next, in the house where she formerly lived, in Smith Street. She undertakes to teach young Ladies reading English with the greatest correctness and propriety, both prose and verse; plain work, Dresden, catgut and all kinds of collar'd work, on canvas and camllet; all

[1] *Pennsylvania Gazette*, May 7, 1747.
[2] *New York Gazette*, June 22, 1747.
[3] *Ibid.*, March 29, 1773.

in the neatest manner and newest taste. She in-
structs them in the strictest principles of religion and
morality and in the most polite behaviour, and takes
the utmost care to instruct them in a perfect knowledge of the subjects they read, (as far as their capacity
can take) and provides the principle part of the books
proper for their improvements at her own expense.
She also takes day scholars, which will have the same
improvement as the boarders. If any that board their
children chuse they should learn the French language,
she will have a master attend at her house.

"As far as their capacity can take"! One perceives
that Sarah Hay possessed one qualification of a
good teacher — a realization of the limitations of
her pupils. But she did not have to pass them by
the regents' examinations.

Every one of these teachers already quoted advertised her readiness to instruct in needlework and
allied subjects. Here, rather than in the three R's,
lay the chief object of these schools for young
ladies. The modern reader is astonished at the
variety of methods by which the colonial gentlewomen could be properly "finished." Here is an
early example: [1]

Martha Gazley, late of Great Britain, now in the
city of New-York, makes and teaches the following
curious Works, viz. Artificial Fruit and Flowers and
other Wax-Work, Nuns-Work, Philligree and Pencil

[1] *New York Gazette*, December 13, 1731.

WAX FIGURE MADE ABOUT 1765 BY SUSANNAH GEE, DAUGHTER OF THE REVEREND JOSHUA GEE, OF THE NORTH CHURCH, BOSTON

Work upon Muslin and all sorts of Needle-Work and
Raising of Paste, as also to Paint upon Glass, and
Transparent for Sconces, with other Works. . . .

These would seem to be sufficient, and one suspects
that perhaps it is as well that Mrs. Gazley, who
lived "at the Widdow Butler's," confined herself to
"Philligree" and so forth, rather than undertaking
to teach spelling.

It would be rash to assert that better opportunities could be offered anywhere than this; but the
girls around Boston had a greater choice of schools
where similar accomplishments were taught, such
as the following: [1]

This may inform young Gentlewomen in Town and
Country, that early in the Spring Mrs. Hiller designs
to open a Boarding-School at the House where she
lives, in Fish-Street, at the North End of Boston, next
Door to Dr. Clark's, where they may be taught Wax-
Work, Transparent and Filligree Painting upon Glass,
Japanning, Quill Work, Feather-Work and Embroidering with Gold and Silver, and several other
sorts of Work not here enumerated, and may be
supplied with Patterns and all sorts of Drawing, and
Materials for their Work.

Mrs. Hiller advertised off and on for some years.
Elinor Purcell, who started a school on Milk Street
in 1755, taught these arts, specializing in embroider-

[1] *Boston Evening Post*, February 1, 1748.

COLONIAL WOMEN OF AFFAIRS

ing coats of arms, and shellwork.[1] Elinor M'Glvaine, "opposite the Governor's," enumerated similar lines, which she grouped as "works proper for young ladies."[2] Elizabeth Cain was the only one of these teachers who specified spinning in her curriculum.[3] Margaret Macklewain, who advertised the dyeing and cleaning of gloves from 1735 to 1753, called attention in 1736 to her pastry school.[4] This is the only example noted of teaching domestic science; and this apparently did not long survive, as it is not referred to in Mrs. Macklewain's later advertisements.

Two school-dames of Philadelphia gave their prices for teaching these intricate subjects. In 1759, Mrs. Anderson charged " 10 Pistoles to those that come to the House; and 15 Pistoles to those Ladies that Chuse to be taught at their own Houses."[5] As a pistole was worth something like four dollars, the price seems high, since board was evidently not included. In 1762, Elizabeth Scharibrook announced a school[6]

for teaching all manner of Berlin or Dresden Needle work in the genteelest and most elegant manner, the

[1] *Boston Evening Post*, April 17, 1755.
[2] *Ibid.*, March 31, 1755.   [3] *Ibid.*, March 27, 1759.
[4] *Ibid.*, November 29, 1736.
[5] *Pennsylvania Gazette*, May 10, 1759.
[6] *Ibid.*, June 24, 1726.

price is 7 Pistoles to learn the whole; Ladies under 12 years of Age taken for 10 shillings entrance and 30 shillings a Quarter.

Undoubtedly prices had risen since Dame Walker was paid ten shillings a year for her whole class; and, as nowadays, gentility and elegance had their market value. It is to be hoped that the difference was not due to a partiality for embroidery over reading and writing, with which one would think that the "ladies under 12 years of age," at least, might have been more profitably occupied.

In colonial times, as to-day, wealthy families, or those living at a great distance from schools, sometimes employed a resident governess. Not much information about this kind of teacher is forthcoming, yet it appears that she was more common proportionately then than she is in this country nowadays. Such advertisements as the following were fairly frequent: [1]

Wants Employment

A woman who would go into any Gentlemen's Family to instruct Children in Reading, Writing, and Arithmetick, also in the use of their Needle. Inquire of the Printer.

And again: [2]

[1] *New York Gazette,* April 25, 1765.
[2] *New York Mercury,* April 27, 1767.

COLONIAL WOMEN OF AFFAIRS

Wanted, a decent middle aged Woman who has been used to the care of Children, she must be able to teach Young Ladies to read, and the use of the Needle.

Indentured servants of the better class sometimes acted as governess. No instances of this kind have been noted in New England, where indentured servants were never so numerous as farther south. The following is from Philadelphia, in 1729:

A likely Young Woman's Time to be disposed of, that can write, Flourish, do Plain-Work, and Mark very well, fit to teach School; by George Brownell, School-Master in Philadelphia.[1]

A pleasant glimpse of an indentured governess is afforded in the "Life of Jane Hoskens, Minister of the Gospel, among the People called Quakers." She came to Philadelphia in 1719, with a family named Davis, who had lent her the money for her passage. To quote her own words:[2]

The principals of four families living in Plymouth, who had several children, agreed to procure a sober young woman, as a school-mistress to instruct them in reading, &c. And on their applying to their friends in town, I was recommended for that service. When we saw each other I perceived it my place to go with them; wherefore, on their paying Davis twelve pounds currency, being the whole of his demand

[1] *American Mercury*, October 9, 1729.
[2] *Friends' Library*, vol. 1, p. 461.

against me, I bound myself to them by indenture for three years, and went cheerfully with them to the aforesaid place. . . . The children learned very fast, which afforded comfort to me and satisfaction to their parents.

It is apparent that pre-Revolutionary women played an important part as elementary teacher, as school-dame in the town school, as mistress of the boarding-school, and as governess. It would be interesting to find a woman teaching in one of the colonial colleges; but no such instance has come to light as yet. This does not mean, however, that women did not render valuable service, even in colleges. The Reverend Edward Holyoke, President of Harvard College, entered in his diary under date of April 22, 1762, "Mrs. Landman began her business as college sexton." [1]

[1] *Holyoke Diaries*, p. 26.

CHAPTER VI

THE LANDED PROPRIETOR

WEALTH and position in the New World, as in most other places, were based on the ownership of land, and from a very early date women shared in this, not only by favor of their men-folk, but in their own right. There are several instances where women served as leaders of groups of settlers. Probably the earliest case is that of Margaret and Mary Brent, who came to Maryland in 1638, bringing nine colonists with them. The sisters took up manors — that is, plantations of a thousand acres or more — and sent back to England for more settlers. The lord of a manor had the right of holding so-called "courts-baron," but only two instances have been found where this right was exercised. One of these was in 1659 at St. Gabriel's manor, the property of Mistress Mary Brent.

A tenant appeared, did fealty to the lady, and took seisin of a messuage of thirty-seven acres by delivery of a rod, "according to the custom of the manor," engaging to pay yearly "fifteen pecks of good Indian corn and one fat capon or a hen and a half; and for a heriot half a barrel of like corn or the value thereof."[1]

[1] Browne, p. 148.

The record does not state what was to become of the other half hen.

Margaret Brent exercised still greater influence. Before his death in 1647, Governor Leonard Calvert appointed Thomas Greene as his successor in office, but made Mistress Brent his sole executor, with the laconic instruction: "Take all and pay all." The estate amounted to only one hundred and ten pounds, and the historian of Maryland remarks:

> In view of subsequent occurrences one is tempted to think that if he had reversed his testamentary dispositions and made Greene his executor and Mistress Brent governor, it would have been, on the whole, a better arrangement.[1]

Leonard Calvert had been attorney for his brother, Lord Baltimore, and with the approval of the court she succeeded to this responsibility. A crisis soon arose, which she met vigorously. The times were troublous, and in order to drive out marauders, Governor Calvert had been obliged to hire quite a body of soldiers for whose payment he had pledged his own and his brother's estates. He died before he could fulfill his contract, and the soldiers threatened mutiny. Mistress Brent succeeded in calming them, and took enough of Lord Baltimore's cattle to make up the necessary

[1] Browne, p. 64.

sum. His lordship, who had had nothing to say about her appointment as his attorney, was not well pleased by her action; but the Assembly wrote him that she had obtained from the soldiers a respect they would have shown to none other, and that without her prompt interference, the colony would have been ruined.

One tribute alone the Assembly withheld. The Archives of Maryland state that on January 21, 1647/48

came Mrs. Margarett Brent and requested to have vote in the howse for herselfe and voyce allso, for that att the last Court 3d Jan. it was ordered that the said Mrs. Brent was to be looked upon and received as his Lps. Attorney. The Govr, denyed that the sd. Mrs. Brent should have any vote in the Howse. And the sd. Mrs. Brent protested against all proceedings in this present Assembly unless shee may be present and have vote as aforesd.

A surprisingly modern sentiment! "Mrs." in those days was used as a title of respect, without regard to marital status. Apparently Margaret Brent never married. Her last recorded appearance was about some property, left her by the will of a disappointed suitor.[1]

Another woman colonizer was Elizabeth Haddon. Her father, John Haddon, a Quaker of Surrey,

[1] *Op. cit.*, and Earle, *Colonial Dames*, pp. 45-48.

England, had acquired title to some land in New
Jersey. In 1701, when Elizabeth was only nineteen
years old, she crossed the water alone to look after
her father's property.   After staying awhile with
co-religionists in Philadelphia, she moved into a
house which she had had built for her on her
father's land, and named the region Haddonfield.
The following year she married John Estaugh, a
minister among the Friends whom she had met in
England and again in Philadelphia. Tradition says
that she was obliged to imitate Priscilla Alden's
method of bringing him to the point. Mrs. Estaugh
had no children of her own, but she adopted one of
her sister's. Throughout her long life, she exercised a leading influence in the community. She
died in 1762, about eighty years old.[1]

In Pennsylvania also a woman figures as one of
the early proprietors. Mary Warenbuer and her
husband John (or Daniel?) Ferree, a silk weaver,
had lived in Lindau, France. Suffering persecution
as Huguenots, they fled with their six children to
Strassburg. Here the husband soon died, and the
management of affairs devolved upon the wife.
When her children were grown, she put through
plans for transporting the whole family and some
friends to America. First they went to England,

[1] Camden, p. 646.

where she obtained an interview with William Penn. He was much interested in her, and not only promised his assistance, but took her to see Queen Anne. After six months in London, the little company joined some French and German settlers who were going to New York. In 1711, Madame Ferree took out a warrant for two thousand acres of land in New Strasburg, Lancaster County, Pennsylvania. This warrant was afterward confirmed to her son Daniel and her son-in-law, Isaac Le Fevre. Madame Ferree died at Conestoga in 1716.[1]

In the same year that Margaret Brent went to Maryland, Anne Hutchinson was the moving spirit (in more senses than one) of a group who journeyed from the comparative security of Massachusetts Bay to the wilderness of Rhode Island, where they established the little town of Portsmouth, from which later sprang Newport. A far cry it seems, from the inspired Puritan woman to the social leaders of modern Newport! Almost a century and a half later, another inspired woman, Ann Lee, led a company of her disciples from England to western New York. These women, however, were colonizers only incidentally; their real significance is as religious leaders.[2]

In all the colonies, women seem to have owned

[1] Fosdick, p. 393 ff.; *Lancaster*, p. 926.   [2] See Chapter VII. B.

THE LANDED PROPRIETOR

land on exactly the same terms as men. Women who possessed large tracts were naturally less common in New England than elsewhere. Elizabeth Poole, one of the rare "old maidens" of early days, is mentioned as the founder of Taunton, Massachusetts,[1] and Abigail Bromfield was one of the proprietors, along with John Hancock, Samuel Adams, and other men, of the undivided land in Maine.[2] And in 1771, the remarkably named Marcy Cheese advertised for sale "the small island of Chopoquidic, adjoining Martha's Vineyard."[3]

It is farther south, however, that the great estates flourished. Many are the women of New Netherland who owned and increased valuable properties. An advertisement in the "New York Gazette" for July 20, 1730, calls to mind a family in which unusual ability made itself manifest from mother to daughter for three generations. This notice is in regard to the sale at auction of the real estate of the late Cornelia DePeyster, and it enumerates the following:

A House and Lot in Broad Street, joyning to the House now building by Mr. Scott,
A House and Lot, joyning the former, in which Mr. Annis lives,

[1] Earle, *Colonial Dames.*
[2] *Boston Evening Post*, October 3, 1768.
[3] *Providence Gazette*, October 20, 1771.

A House and Lot joyning thereunto, wherein Mrs. DePeyster lives,

A House and Lot adjoyning, wherein John Anthony lives,

A Lot on Mill Street, near the Jews' Synagogue,

A House and Lot on Beaver street, which reaches back to Petticoat Lane,

A Lot on Queen street.

Not a bad bit of property, even if real estate in New York was worth less then than now. Mrs. DePeyster, as Cornelia Lubbetse, had come to New Amsterdam in 1651, to join her betrothed, Johannes DePeyster; and she had died in 1725, over ninety years of age. Throughout her long life she had played a prominent part in the town. She is credited with responsibility for the first cargo of salt brought to the colony — an important article, before local methods of production had been discovered.

Mrs. DePeyster's elder daughter, Maria, married a young merchant named Schrick, who owned property in Hartford and Flushing as well as in New York. He died shortly after the marriage, and the youthful widow carried on his business in her own name. She soon remarried, the second husband being a Scotchman named Spratt. After ten years he died also, leaving her again a widow, this time with four young children. Her mother and sister aided her to carry on her double business inheritance but three years later she married her third husband, a widower with many children. It is hardly surprising that the much-married lady died herself in the following year, 1700, at the age of forty-one.

The Spratt children were brought up by their Grandmother DePeyster. The daughter, Mary Spratt, was married when only about seventeen to Samuel Provoost, a successful young importer. The "Dictionary of National Biography" says he had made a fortune by smuggling. Mary's money was partly invested in the business — whatever it was — and she assisted in the management. This was fortunate, for after a few years she was left a widow, with two young children. Thereupon, according to the dictionary aforesaid, "the lady began a provision business of a lawful kind." She had a row of offices built in front of her house. Her counting-house was on a side street, and, in order to encourage business, she had flat stones laid along her property, and up to the streets on either side. This was the first sidewalk in New York, and it is said to have attracted visitors from far and wide. It may have been one reason why the business flourished, for flourish it did, and was continued after her second marriage, in 1722, to James Alexander. On one occasion during the French and Indian wars

COLONIAL WOMEN OF AFFAIRS

Mrs. Alexander received the contract to supply provisions for the King's troops. Mr. and Mrs. Alexander were people of great influence in the colony. After a few years, Mrs. Alexander bought a country place at Perth Amboy, which a writer of the times tells us could be reached in "a short voyage of less than three days from New York." Here Mrs. Alexander took great interest in the welfare of her Indian neighbors, among whom she gained fame as a medicine-woman. James Alexander died in 1756, and his wife in 1760. Their son William asserted his title as sixth Earl of Stirling; nevertheless, he continued his mother's business in his native land. During the Revolution, he took an active and useful part on the American side, and became a general.[1]

An advertisement in Zenger's Journal for March 10, 1735, announced that two houses, one large and one small, and seventeen lots of land, belonging to the estate of the late Catharina Philipse, would be sold at auction by her executors, Philip and Frederick Van Cortland. This was undoubtedly the widow Catharina Duval, born Van Cortland, who married Frederick Philipse in 1694. Mrs. Philipse had been intensely interested in the welfare of the Indians, and she provided a school for them, and had

[1] Van Rensselaer; *Dictionary of National Biography.*

106

a church built near her manor-house. It is said that she personally superintended its construction, riding over every day on her gray mare. She endowed these charitable projects with a considerable part of her fortune.

Frederick Philipse was a widower when he married Catharina Van Cortland, and his first wife, Margaret Hardenbroeck, has been called "perhaps the most enterprising of all the Dutch colonists, male or female." She came to the New World when quite young, with her first husband, Peter De Vries; they bought a plantation on Staten Island and began a settlement there. After the death of De Vries, his widow sold this property and invested the money in ships, with which she established what was probably the first packet line between Europe and America. Mrs. De Vries went repeatedly as supercargo, in order to superintend the buying and selling. She fell in love with Frederick Philipse on one of these trips when he was a passenger taking a stock of furs to be sold in Europe. After her remarriage in 1661, Mrs. Philipse continued her business. The combined industry of husband and wife made them the richest couple in New Amsterdam, and they bought large holdings around what is now Yonkers, which was erected into "The Philipse Manor," besides considerable property in Manhattan. Margaret Philipse died about 1690.

A diary kept by the Labbadist missionaries who came to America in 1679, gives a not wholly flattering side-light on Mrs. Philipse's industry. These men sailed from Holland "in a small flute ship, of which Thomas Singleton was master, but the superior authority over both ship and cargo was in Margaret Philipse, who was the owner of both, and with whom we agreed for our passage from Amsterdam to New York, in New Netherland, at 75 guelders for each person, payable in Holland." Mrs. Philipse was not on the ship when it sailed, but she overtook it in her own yacht, and came on board with her husband and daughter, and two servants. Unfortunately, according to the diarists, the passengers suffered greatly from overcrowding and filth, and they accuse the owner of avarice.[1]

Another Dutchwoman of affairs was Mrs. Cornelia Schuyler, the mother of General Philip Schuyler of Revolutionary fame. Her father was Stephanus Van Cortland. In the division of the manor estate, her share came to more than seven thousand acres. This amount she increased; on one occasion, after the death of her husband, she took out a patent for thirteen hundred acres.[2]

[1] Van Rensselaer; Wharton.   [2] Humphrey, pp. 29, 78.

THE LANDED PROPRIETOR

Women in the Southern States also owned and managed huge plantations. Mrs. Elizabeth Digges possessed one hundred and eight negro slaves, apparently the greatest number held by any one person in seventeenth-century Virginia; according to current prices, these must have been worth about twenty-four hundred pounds. The inventory of Mrs. Digges's estate, presented in 1699, shows her to have had a lavishly furnished house, according to the standards of the day. One chest, for instance, contained one hundred and twenty-six napkins, and sixty tablecloths. Her silver plate amounted to two hundred and sixty-one ounces. Her hall parlor contained five tables, twenty chairs, two couches, two pairs of brass andirons, and one clock. To set off this magnificence, hung on the walls were five pictures, valued at one shilling apiece! Throughout the mansion, the contents of which are meticulously itemized, not a single book is mentioned.[1]

Plenty of women dealt in land on a smaller scale. Rebecca Wells, of Philadelphia, was apparently an early real estate agent; for instance, on January 20, 1757, she advertises two lots of land for sale and a house for rent.[2]

For over twenty years, Mrs. Sarah Boylston,

[1] Bruce, pp. 88, 174, 182.   [2] *Pennsylvania Gazette.*

of Boston, inserts occasional advertisements of property to rent. The location noted in most of them is "near Faneuil Hall," and it may be that the "large brick dwelling-house," the "convenient dwelling-house," and so forth, were all the same, and that for some reason her tenants changed often. On her last appearance, however, in the "Boston Evening Post" for January 28, 1765, she is advertising as to let "a very Convenient Dwelling-House and Gardens, together with about 15 Acres of land, near Col Joseph Williams's in Roxbury," and this time she gives her address "near Faneuil Hall." Perhaps she had given the large brick house up for renting purposes, and had gone to live in it herself.

Some methods of stimulating business appear to have been in good and regular standing in colonial days, which would hardly be smiled upon in our own time. The "Pennsylvania Gazette" for April 25, 1745, has the following notice:

To be set up by way of Lottery, by Nicholas Bishop and Hester his Wife, 70 odd Lots in Wilmington; each subscriber paying 4 shillings in Hand, and 2 shillings a year Ground-Rent. There are no blanks, but all Prizes. The Lottery will be drawn the 16th of May in this City.

No need, evidently, to look the ground over beforehand. These colonial Bishops hardly require points from Babbit.

Women worked the land, as well as traded in it — and perhaps worked their customers. The records of the Quarterly Courts of Essex County give numerous glimpses of women about Salem who were wresting a livelihood from the land. In September, 1648, Widow Luce Waite sued Samuel Greenfield for debt, for 1460 pipe-staves which she had furnished him, at three pounds per thousand. The defendant appealed. Pipe-staves were the cause of controversy again in 1653, when Thomas King sued Edward Colcord for not having delivered 1400 to the Widow Chase; defendant acknowledged judgment to the plaintiff. The next year Widow Chase appeared in her own behalf, charging Christopher Palmer with running a ditch through her meadow; judgment for the plaintiff. In 1658, Widow Margaret Scott accused Richard Shatswell of trespass, for ploughing up her land and felling trees and causing trees to be felled on her ground. In 1664, Widow Susan Rogers received a verdict against Mr. Philip Nelson, for having interfered with her meadow of forty acres, taking away ten loads of hay which she had had cut.

Mrs. John Davenport, wife of the minister of New Haven, looked after the extensive property interests of John Winthrop, the younger, when political business kept him in England.[1] The correspondence between Governor Winthrop and Mr. Davenport is filled with messages in regard to the management of the iron-works, payments for supplies, receipts for produce, employment of workmen, and so forth, all attended to by Mrs. Davenport. She had some amusing difficulties, not unknown in other times; her husband, in a letter to Winthrop dated "Newhaven, this 22 of the 9th, 1655," wrote:

My wife had a man in pursuite that would be very fitt to manage your Island, if a marriage, which he is about, doth not hinder.

It is rather astonishing to discover a Puritan divine conniving at his wife's pursuit of another man; but the object here was laudable. Governor Winthrop was in need of a competent manager for Fisher's Island, "against the mouth of the Pequot River," which had been granted to him in 1640.

Farmers or plantation owners naturally did not advertise their wares like merchants or tavern-keepers; but they used the papers constantly to announce the dereliction of an indentured servant, slave, or horse, or now and then the finding of a

[1] Waters, p. 48; *Mass. Hist. Coll.*, 4th Ser., vol. VII, pp. 492 ff.

stray animal. The servants and live stock of New England seem a little less migratory than elsewhere, but even here they were open to reproach. In many of the journals from farther south, the bulk of the advertising is of this nature, and these brief items give glimpses of many women who managed plantations, and sometimes indicate the variety of home industries which they conducted. Thus, Mrs. Christine Eltington, of Somerset County, East New Jersey, advertised in the "New York Gazette" for November 10, 1729, the loss of two servant men, one a weaver and one a cooper; she would pay four pounds reward for the return of both.

Four years later, in the same paper, Judith Vincent, at Mount Pleasant, Monmouth County, East New Jersey, advertised that her "Indian Fellow named Stoffil" had run away; he a cooper and carpenter by trade. She offered three pounds reward and charges. Coopers seemed to be particularly elusive, but horses were almost as bad. In one issue of the "Providence Gazette," November 29, 1771, Alice Philbrook, of Cumberland, offered five dollars reward for the return of a stolen mare — ten dollars if the thief be caught; and Marcy Dexter, of North Providence, offered three dollars and six dollars for a horse, ditto. Notices of this sort are legion.

COLONIAL WOMEN OF AFFAIRS

Several women owned and managed wharves. The "Essex County Gazette" for August 30, 1768, gave notice of the sale of a schooner of 120 tons, "now laying at Mrs. Hodges's Wharf." Wharves frequently served as the prototype of our employment bureaus, although under an unpleasant aspect. Thus, the "American Mercury" in the fall of 1725 announced:

> A Choice Parcel of Men Servants and one Woman to be sold, on Board the Ship Lovely, now lying at the Wharf of the Widdow Allen, at 12 to 14 pounds per head, also very good Gloucester Cheese, at Eightpence a Pound.

In 1730, the same paper mentioned Widow Hun's wharf in a similar connection. In the "Boston Evening Post" for November 28, 1763, Mrs. Knox at Bull Wharf advertised seven indented maids to dispose of.

Some of the women named in these brief newspaper advertisements may have been merely carrying on the farm work of a dead husband or father, without any real initiative in the matter; the information is usually too brief to settle this point. There are not a few women, however, about whom more knowledge is available, and who certainly showed a commendable degree of enterprise. Such a woman was Hannah Dubre (or Dubrey, or Du-

114

berry, for the records allow a choice), who thus first addressed the public through the "Pennsylvania Gazette," in the fall of 1753:

To be sold by Hannah Dubre, living in the Northern Liberties, next plantation to Capt Peal's, within two miles of Philadelphia, ... All sorts of seeds either wholesale or retail, at very reasonable rates.

By the next issue, the distance had grown to two miles and a half; otherwise the statement was practically the same, and it was inserted several times nearly every autumn for the next fifteen years, and occasionally in the spring. Sometimes shops in town were named where the seeds might be bought, if would-be purchasers were discouraged by the two and one half miles. Numerous women shopkeepers sold imported seeds, but this is the only woman noted who sold seeds which she herself grew. In February, 1770, Mrs. Dubre advertised her plantation for sale, thirty-three acres with fruit orchard, kitchen garden, asparagus beds, and a house with good kitchen, and a pump before the door. This, no doubt, was "modern conveniences" at that time.

Mrs. Grant, of Laggan, a Scotchwoman who lived in the colonies, chiefly New York State, from 1760 to 1768, says that "not only the training of children but of plants ... was the female province." [1]

Grant, p. 46.

COLONIAL WOMEN OF AFFAIRS

I think I yet see, what I have so often beheld both in town and country, a respectable mistress of a family going out to her garden, in an April morning, with her great calash, her little painted basket of seed, and her rake over her shoulder, to her garden labors. These were by no means figurative.

"From morn till noon, from noon till dewy eve,"

A woman in very easy circumstances, and abundantly gentle in form and manners, would sow, and plant, and rake, incessantly.

Another Scotchwoman, Janet Schaw, who spent some time in the Southern States shortly before the Revolution, pictures such a woman who put her skill to good use. Writing in Wilmington, North Carolina, in the spring of 1775, she speaks of a particularly attractive estate which she had seen, and continues: [1]

They tell me, however, that the Mrs. of this place is a pattern of industry, and that the house and everything in it was the product of her labors. She has (it seems) a garden, from which she supplies the town with what vegetables they use, also with mellons and other fruits. She even descends to make minced pies, tarts, and cheese-cakes, and little biskets, which she sends down to town once or twice a day, beside her eggs, poultry, and butter, and she is the only one who continues to have Milk. They tell me she is an agreeable woman, and I am sure she has

[1] Schaw, p. 178.

116

good sense, from one circumstance, — all her little commodities are contrived so as not to exceed one penny a piece, and her customers know she will not run tick, which were they to run by the length of sixpence, must be the case, as that is a sum not in everybody's power, and she must be paid by some other articles, whereas the two coppers, (that is, half pence) are ready money. I am sure I would be happy in such an acquaintance. But this is impossible; her husband is at best a brute by all accounts and is beside the president of the committee and the instigator of the cruel and unjust treatment the friends of government are experiencing at present.

A note states that this was Mary, the wife of Cornelius Harnet, who owned a big plantation named Hilton, near Wilmington. Mrs. Harnet died in New York City, April 19, 1792. Her husband was a prominent patriot. He may not have been a brute — Miss Schaw was prejudiced against patriots anyway — but the editor inclines to the opinion that he was not a particularly estimable man.

A good many people nowadays would have a fellow-feeling on financial matters with the natives of Wilmington; but a place where one could get a "minced pie" or an egg, not to mention poultry, which perhaps Miss Schaw overlooked, for two coppers, sounds like Eldorado.

Several colonial women attained distinction as

botanists. Foremost among these is Jane Colden, the daughter of Cadwalader Colden, Lieutenant-Governor of New York. He had had an excellent education in Europe, and was a man of high scientific attainments. He taught his daughter the recently published system of Linnæus, and both she and her father corresponded with the Swedish naturalist. An English botanist wrote about her to Linnæus:

This young lady merits your esteem and does honor to your system. She has drawn and described four hundred plants in your method. Her father has a plant called after him, "Coldenia." Suppose you should call this (referring to a new genus) "Coldenella," or any other name that might distinguish her in your genera.

A more intimate glimpse of her is given in a letter written by a young Scotchman, William Rutherfurd, describing a visit to Dr. Colden's home:

His daughter Jenny is a Florist, and a Botanist. She has discovered a great number of plants never before described, and has given them Properties and Virtues, many of which are found useful in Medicine and she draws and colors them with great beauty.
N.B. She makes the best cheese I ever ate in America.

The versatile Jenny married Dr. William Farquhar

in 1759, and died seven years later, when about forty-two years old.[1]

In 1741, a nineteen-year-old girl in South Carolina wrote to a friend:

> I have planted a figg orchard, with design to dry them, and export them. I have reckoned my expence and the prophets to arise from these figgs, but was I to tell you how great an Estate I am to make this way, and how 'tis to be laid out, you would think me far gone in romance. Y[r] good Uncle I know has long thought I have a fertile brain for schemeing, I only confirm him in his opinion; but I own I love the vegitable world extreamly.

No one, man or woman, of the colonial period benefited his country more through loving "the vegitable world extreamly" than the youthful writer, Eliza Lucas.

Eliza's father, George Lucas, a British army officer, must have been a man of uncommon sense, with advanced ideas regarding the sphere of women. He encouraged his daughter to read French and Virgil, and disapproved of fancy-work. About 1737 or 1738 he bought a plantation in South Carolina, hoping to settle down there as a gentleman farmer; but the renewal of war with Spain forced him to rejoin his command at Antigua. Mrs. Lucas was

[1] Van Rensselaer, pp. 258, 259.

in very delicate health, and she remained on the plantation with her children. The oldest, Eliza, then only seventeen years old, was left in charge. This was no sinecure, for beside attending to the routine work and acting as school-mistress for her younger sister and some of the negro children, she devoted herself to problems of experimental agriculture. Her earliest memorandum on this subject which has been preserved was written in July, 1739:

> I wrote my father a very long letter on his planta-
> tion affairs, . . . on the pains I had taken to bring the
> Indigo, Ginger, Cotton, Lucern, and Cassada to per-
> fection, and had greater hopes from the Indigo —
> if I could have the seed earlier the next year from the
> East Indies — than any of ye rest of ye things I had
> tryd, . . . also concerning pitch and tarr and lime and
> other plantation affairs.

In those days it was of vital importance for every colony to produce something which was valuable to Europe; in no other way could it obtain the manufactured articles which were essential to its own progress. So far, rice had been the only profitable crop in South Carolina, and that could not be grown on the higher land.

The cultivation of indigo is a complicated and delicate process. The overseer whom Colonel

Lucas sent over from the East Indies, unwilling to raise up a rival to his native island, contrived to spoil one year's crop, and laid the blame, of course, on the climate. Still Miss Lucas persevered with her experiments, and she was completely successful. One source of difficulty had been to get seeds from the East Indies early enough to suit the season, and in 1744 Miss Lucas devoted her entire crop to making seed, which she gave to any of the neighboring planters who would undertake to grow it. As the seed was worth about ten pounds a bushel, this showed a good deal of public spirit. Among her neighbors were a number of Huguenots who had seen indigo growing in France, and they were particularly successful with it. Enough was raised so that in 1747 they began to export it to England. The mother country was so glad to receive indigo from a colony of her own, instead of importing it from the French colonies, that she immediately offered a bounty of sixpence a pound. This made indigo-raising extremely profitable, and until the Revolution it remained the chief product of the highlands of Carolina. Before 1800, it was superseded, and finally abandoned entirely, in favor of cotton, the cultivation of which became more profitable after the invention of the cotton gin.

In 1744, while the experiments with indigo were

progressing, Miss Lucas married Charles Pinckney, of Charleston, later chief justice of South Carolina, a widower many years her senior, but a man of ability and congenial tastes, to whom she was thoroughly devoted. Mrs. Pinckney had two sons and a daughter, and her agricultural pursuits were intermingled with educational experiments. In a letter describing her eldest child, she wrote to a friend in England:

> Shall I give you the trouble my dear Madam to buy him the new toy (a description of which I enclose) to teach him according to Mr. Lock's method (wch I have carefully studied) to play himself into learning. Mr. Pinckney himself has been contriving a sett of toys to teach him his letters by the time he can speak, you perceive we begin by times for he is not yet four months old.

The victim of this eighteenth-century Montessori method expressed the opinion that it was "sad stuff"; but at any rate it did him no harm. There is no record, however, of such advanced pedagogy being applied to Mrs. Pinckney's younger children.

Agricultural interests were not neglected during these years. Shortly after Mrs. Pinckney's marriage her mother and the other children joined their father in Antigua, and Mrs. Pinckney kept up a general supervision of her father's plantation, as

MRS. ELIZA PINCKNEY TO HER HUSBAND

Sent by messenger to Charleston in June or July, 1744

well as shared in the direction of one owned by her husband. Her correspondence tells of experiments with hemp and flax. These were not permanently successful; but progress was made in teaching cotton- and wool-weaving. Furthermore, Mrs. Pinckney undertook on her husband's plantation the cultivation of silk. Although this did not prove as profitable as the indigo-raising, Mrs. Pinckney produced enough raw silk to have three handsome gowns woven from it, one of which is still preserved by her descendants.

In the spring of 1752, business took Mr. Pinckney to England, and his wife and children accompanied him. Mrs. Pinckney has left an interesting account of their gracious reception by the Dowager Princess of Wales, to whom she presented one of the silk dresses before mentioned. The family stayed in England until 1758, and then left the two little boys in school there. Only a few weeks after their return, Mr. Pinckney died, and his widow was left again with heavy responsibilities. Her husband had owned land and negroes in various parts of the colony, and the years following 1758, filled with the French and Indian War, and then troubles with the mother country, were difficult ones for landowners. Mrs. Pinckney had had too much experience, however, to be overwhelmed now. Her sons, Charles Cotesworth Pinckney and Thomas Pinckney, did not return until a few years before the Revolutionary War, in which, notwithstanding their English affiliations, they took an active part on the American side. This is not the place to review their distinguished careers, but it is interesting to recall that the elder was the American commissioner to the French Republic who is credited with giving utterance to the sentiment: "Millions for defense, but not one cent for tribute."

During the war, Mrs. Pinckney's two sons and her son-in-law were in active service; and there was plenty of call for heroism and skill on the part of their women-folk. She lived to see peace established, and to aid her daughter in welcoming Washington to her home in 1791. In April, 1793, she went to Philadelphia, hoping to get medical aid in a severe illness. She recovered enough to gain pleasure from the visits of many old friends, but she died quite suddenly on May 26th. President Washington, by his own request, acted as a pall-bearer. She lies buried in St. Peter's Churchyard in Philadelphia.[1]

The substantial contribution which Mrs. Pinckney made to the prosperity of South Carolina, through the establishment of indigo-raising, has

[1] Ravenel.

124

been described. A greater contribution to the welfare of her country lies in the careers of her distinguished descendants.

It may well be that Mrs. Pinckney was preeminent among colonial women landowners; at any rate, we know more about her achievements. But it is probable that women, unnoticed by their contemporaries and unknown to posterity, through management of the land shared more in building up this country than in any other way.

CHAPTER VII

WITH TONGUE, PEN, AND PRINTER'S INK

A. Authors

"I am obnoxious to each carping tongue
Who says my hand a needle better fits,
A poet's pen all scorn I should thus wrong;
For such despite they cast on female wits,
If what I do prove well, it won't advance —
They'll say it's stolen, or else it was by chance." [1]

THUS Anne Bradstreet, the first American poet, complained of the current attitude toward the literary production of women. She herself was no extreme feminist, but admitted, to a degree that many modern women would find irritating, that men's preëminent merits in all lines were unquestionable; she asked from men only "some small acknowledgement of ours." Regarding her own efforts, Mrs. Bradstreet is genuinely modest, and she concludes the poem from which the stanza above is taken thus:

"And oh, ye high flown quills that soar the skies,
And ever with your prey still catch your praise,
If e'er you deign these lowly lines your eyes,
Give thyme or parsley wreath; I ask no bays.
This mean and unrefin'd ore of mine
Will make your glistering gold but more to shine." [2]

[1] Bradstreet, p. 8.   [2] Ibid.

THE GOVERNOR SIMON BRADSTREET HOUSE IN NORTH ANDOVER
Where Anne Bradstreet lived

WITH TONGUE AND PEN

Mrs. Bradstreet was born in England in 1612, the daughter of Thomas Dudley. At the age of sixteen, she married Simon Bradstreet, and with him and her father came to the New World in 1630. Bradstreet was destined to become governor of the colony, but this was many years later, after the death of his wife. He had a farm in Andover, and Mrs. Bradstreet shared to the full the hardships of pioneer days as a farmer's wife. It was at Andover that her eight children were born. Add to the care of her family and household the fact that she suffered from considerable ill-health, and one is filled with amazement that a woman so situated ever wrote a line.

It is common enough for authors to protest that they had not intended to publish their books; but in Mrs. Bradstreet's case this was a fact. Apparently she had allowed her poems to circulate among her friends, and her brother-in-law, going to England, obtained possession of the manuscripts and had them published in London. In the preface which he wrote, he says that he fears the displeasure of no one except the author, without whose knowledge he was acting. After admitting that the reader would not believe it is possible a woman should have done so excellently, he gives this pleasant characterization of her:

COLONIAL WOMEN OF AFFAIRS

It is the work of a woman, honored and esteemed where she lives for her gracious demeanor, her eminent parts, her pious conversation, her courteous disposition, her exact diligence in her place, and discreet managing of her family occasions; and more than so, these poems are the fruit of but some few hours curtailed from sleep and other refreshments. [1]

The editor, hoping perhaps to turn aside any disapproval of his act, secured introductory verses from several friends, in which they praise the author; but the pleasure of receiving such praise must have been lessened by their derogatory comments regarding the usual efforts of women. They might have sought some other way of complimenting Mrs. Bradstreet, had they read more carefully the following lines, in a poem addressed to Queen Elizabeth: [2]

> "Nay say, have women worth, or have they none?
> Or had they some, but with our queen it's gone?
> Nay masculines, you have thus taxed us long,
> But she, though dead, will vindicate our wrong.
> Let such as say our sex is void of reason
> Know 'tis a slander now, but once was treason."

Many of Mrs. Bradstreet's poems testify that her brother-in-law's characterization of her was justified. Several addressed to her husband breathe the most devoted love. Take these lines for example: [3]

[1] Bradstreet, p. 3.   [2] *Ibid.*, p. 241.   [3] *Ibid.*, p. 270.

WITH TONGUE AND PEN

"If ever two were one, then surely we,
    If ever man was loved by wife, then thee;
    If ever wife was happy in a man,
    Compare with me, ye women, if ye can."

The references to her children are no less affectionate. In a letter written to them, to be read after her death, she says: [1]

It pleased God to keep me a long time without a child, which was a great grief to me, and cost me many prayers and tears before I obtained one.

Nor was she indifferent to the household cares and pleasures which fill so large a place in the life of the ordinary woman. Few lines that she wrote will appeal more strongly to the feminine heart than these from a poem regarding the burning of her house in 1666: [2]

"Here stood that trunk, and there that chest;
    There lay that store I counted best;
    My pleasant things in ashes lie,
    And them behold no more shall I.
    Under thy roof no guest shall sit,
    Nor at thy table eat a bit;

"No pleasant tale shall e'er be told,
    Nor things recounted done of old;
    No candle e'er shall shine in thee,
    Nor bridegroom's voice e'er heard shall be.
    In silence shalt thou ever lie.
    Adieu, adieu; all's vanity."

---

[1] Bradstreet, p. 315.   [2] *Ibid.*, p. 344.

Other quotations, as interesting as those given, might be made from Mrs. Bradstreet's works. Yet it must be admitted that the bulk of her poetry seems to modern taste a dreary waste of moralizing. It should be borne in mind, however, that the level of poetic taste at the time, in England as well as in the New World, was low, and it would have taken a genius to have risen altogether above it. Mrs. Bradstreet was not a genius; but she was unquestionably the best poet America produced for a good many years, probably for more than a century. It is curious that the first American poet should have been a woman. It was perhaps a good augury for the women of succeeding generations that she should have pleaded woman's cause with such clearness and force, while exemplifying a dignity and sweetness of character which disarmed the most captious critic. Whatever one may think of her poetry, she herself remains a significant and wholly attractive personality. It is pleasant to know that Richard Henry Dana and Oliver Wendell Holmes trace descent from her.[1]

One of the most interesting groups of writings in the Colonial period were the narratives of captivity among the Indians; perhaps the best of them all is

[1] The account of Mrs. Bradstreet's life is based on Norton's Introduction, Bradstreet, pp. vi–xxxii.

the earliest, — that written by Mrs. Mary Rowlandson.

The Reverend Joseph Rowlandson, whom Mary
White married in 1657, was the first settled minister
of Lancaster, Massachusetts. During King Philip's
War the town was alarmed by rumors of an im-
pending attack by the Indians, and Mr. Rowlandson had gone to Boston to beg help from the Council. On February 10, 1675/6, while he was gone,
the attack took place. The entire town was burned
to the ground, many of the inhabitants were killed,
and the rest, about twenty, were captured, among
them Mrs. Rowlandson and her three children,
fourteen, twelve, and six years old. Mrs. Rowlandson and the youngest child had both been wounded,
and the little one died on February 29th. The two
older children were not allowed to stay with their
mother, and she saw them only a few times during
her captivity.

For nearly three months they were kept moving about on long marches through northwest-
ern Massachusetts and southern New Hampshire
and Vermont, as their Indian captors wandered
to escape from the pursuing English troops, or to
plan new attacks. During this time Mr. Rowlandson was trying to get news of his family. One
day in April, when near the town of Athol, Mrs.

Rowlandson received her first direct intimation of this, which she tells of thus: [1]

We began this Remove with wading over Baquag River: the water was up to the knees, and the stream very swift, and so cold that I thought it would have cut me in sunder. — Then I sat down to put on my stockins and shoes, with the tears running down mine eyes, and many sorrowfull thoughts in my heart, but I gat up to go along with them. Quickly there came up to us an Indian, who informed them, that I must go to Wachusit to my master, for there was a Letter come from the Council to the Saggamores, about redeeming the captives, and that there would be another in fourteen dayes, and that I must be there ready. My heart was so heavy before that I could scarce speak or go in the path; and yet now so light, that I could run. My strength seemed to come again, and recruit my feeble knees, and aking heart; yet it pleased them to go but one mile that night, and there we stayed two days.

The negotiations were somewhat protracted, but were finally concluded on May 2d, through the instrumentality of John Hoar, of Concord. Mrs. Rowlandson was soon reunited to her husband, but their joy was mixed with apprehension for their children. Both these were returned to them before long, however. Mrs. Rowlandson bears grateful testimony to the kindness and generosity of those who helped them — the Boston people who raised

[1] Rowlandson, p. 66.

A
NARRATIVE

OF THE

CAPTIVITY, SUFFERINGS AND REMOVES

OF

Mrs. *Mary Rowlandson,*

Who was taken Prifoner by the INDIANS with feveral others,
and treated in the moft barbarous and cruel Manner by thofe
vile Savages : With many other remarkable Events during her
TRAVELS.

Written by her own Hand, for her private Ufe, and now made
public at the earneft Defire of fome Friends, and for the Benefit of the afflicted.

BOSTON

Printed and Sold at JOHN BOYLE's Printing Office, next Door
to the *Three Doves* in Marlborough Street. 1773.

her ransom of twenty pounds, those of Portsmouth who paid her son's ransom of seven pounds, others who hired a house for them, and gave them furniture. Mr. Rowlandson soon received a call to the church at Weathersfield, Connecticut, where he died suddenly in 1678. The church voted an annual allowance of thirty pounds to Mrs. Rowlandson. The date of her death is not known.

Mrs. Rowlandson's narrative has been published in at least thirty editions, the first in Boston in 1682, and the second in London the same year. The subject is one which was of vital interest in its day, and which still grips the heart. Mrs. Rowlandson makes no pretension to style, and displays no learning save in the Bible; but she writes clearly and forcibly, in vigorous and idiomatic English. She was a close observer, and gives valuable information in regard to the habits of the Indians. Her little book is a contribution to the literature of her time of which American women may well be proud.

A later and more willing woman traveler, Madam Sarah Knight, has been mentioned more than once; the extracts already given from her pen show the vigor and vivacity with which she wrote. She appears to have written solely for her own amusement, sometimes, like Silas Wegg, dropping into poetry. The journey was far from easy, and she gave full expression to her fears and discomforts, but with a humor one would hardly have expected from a Puritan schoolmarm — a humor which at times would most certainly have shocked the Puritans of an earlier generation. Take the following, with its unreverential Biblical reference: [1]

Having crossed Providence Ferry, we came to a River wch they Generally Ride thro'. But I dare not venture; so the Post got a Ladd and Cannoo to carry me to tother side, and he rid thro' and Led my hors. The Cannoo was very small and shallow, so that when we were in she seem'd redy to take in water, which greatly terrified me, and caused me to be very circumspect, sitting with my hands fast on each side, my eyes stedy, not daring so much as lodge my tongue a hair's breadth more on one side of my mouth than tother, nor so much as think on Lott's wife, for a wry thought would have oversett our wherey; but was soon put out of this pain, by feeling the Cannoo on shore, wch I as soon almost saluted with my feet; and Rewarding my sculler, again mounted and made the best of our way forwards.

Religious writings were extremely popular in the Colonial days; women were at a disadvantage in the matter of publishing sermons, but they seem to have contributed a fair share of the religious meditations of the time. The "New York Journal" for

[1] Knight, p. 26.

WITH TONGUE AND PEN

January 17, 1736, carried a modest proposal of one such work:

A spiritual Journey Temporaliz'd.
The whole to contain about 8 sheets.

The following Lines, which I received with the Copy, may in some manner give an idea of the Thing itself,

To gain Profit by the enriching of our Minds with wholesome Knowledge, and thereby to better our lives, are the only true Ends of reading Books; and these Ends may be acquired by every generous Peruser of this small Manual, who will at the same time excuse some Incongruities, Mis-spellings, Mis-syntaxes, and Unaptnesses therein contained; to do which he will be the more inclin'd from a Consideration of the Circumstances of the Author, who is a Widow altogether unlearned, and expresses her Thoughts, altho' not on the pinnacle of Politeness, yet in a Dialect not in the least Contemptible. It is a Widow who has run through various Fortunes in Life that here throws in her Mite; the Product of her own Experiences, being desirous that others should avoid the Rocks, Shoals, and Quicksands upon which she herself has struck; and this she Cautions, in a Manner very engaging to the Reader, alluring and captivating the Fancy, and at the same Time surprisingly instructing the Mind; therein following the old adage,

"She wins the Prize, and hits the White,
Who mixes Profit with Delight."

Subscriptions will be taken in by the Printer hereof, at 2d. per Sheet, on good Paper, and a fair character,

135

and good Encouragement will be given to those who subscribe for Numbers to retail.

This tract was not published until 1742; unfortunately no copy of it has been found.

Better fortune has attended another edifying work by a female author, which was printed both in New York and in London in 1750; the "Pennsylvania Gazette" of May 10, 1750, advertised the London edition, while the "Boston Evening Post" for May 10, 1750, announced:

Just printed at New York
And sold by the Publisher of the Paper,

Meditations on Divine Subjects: by Mrs. Mary Lloyd, to which is prefixed an Account of her Life and Character,

by E. Pemberton.

N.B. This Gentlewoman was formerly Consort of the Reverend Ebenezer Pemberton, and afterwards of John Campbell, Esq., both of this Town.

One might think that Mrs. Lloyd's matrimonial experiences would have supplied her with material for interesting meditations. Judge Sewall's diary gives numerous glimpses of her as Mrs. Pemberton, when she seems to have been kindly disposed to lovers in general. Thus, in 1713: [1]

[1] Sewall, vol. ii, p. 378.

Asked her what people thought of my Son's Court-ship; she spake well of it; — commended Mrs. Betty.

And in 1719, when the Judge was courting his second wife; [1]

Visited Madam Pemberton to inquire after Judith. She applauded my Courting Mrs. Tilley: I thank'd her for her Favour in Maintaining what I did.

Unfortunately, when it came to writing, Mrs. Lloyd did not condescend to mundane subjects. The headings of the Meditations are quite enough for the modern reader:

Meditation I. Upon the Truth of the Christian Religion, and an Enquiry into the State of my own Soul.
II. On the Excellency and Advantage of the Christian Religion.
III. On the Suitableness of Jesus Christ, to the Circumstances of Apostate Sinners.

Mrs. Jane Turrell, daughter of the Reverend Benjamin Colman, of Boston, wrote poems in the early part of the eighteenth century which were greeted with considerable favor by her contemporaries, although to modern taste they seem wholly lacking in originality. Her husband published a laudatory memoir of her, shortly after her

1 Sewall, vol. III, p. 228.

early death in 1735, aged only twenty-seven years. The following quatrain is a sufficient sample of her style: [1]

"Phœbus has thrice his yearly Circuit run,
  The Winter's over, and the Summer's done,
Since that *bright Day* on which our Hands were join'd,
  And to Philander I my all resign'd."

The art of timeliness in publication is not altogether a new invention. The colonial papers of 1756 carried the following advertisement: [2]

Just Published,

A Narrative of the Sufferings and surprising Deliverances of William and Elizabeth Fleming, who were taken Captive by Captain Jacob, commander to the Indians, who lately made the Incursions on the Frontiers of Pennsylvania, as related by themselves. Psalm 3, 4, I cried unto the Lord and He heard me, — A Narrative necessary to be read by all who are going in the present Expedition, as well as every British subject, wherein it fully appears, that the Barbarities of the Indians is owing to the French, and chiefly their Priests.

Mr. and Mrs. Fleming were separated after their capture, and each tells of his or her own adventures. Their captivity was not long, and the account of it is greatly inferior in interest to that of Mrs. Rowlandson.

[1] Turrell, p. 103.
[2] *Boston Evening Post*, April 19, 1756.

WITH TONGUE AND PEN

Many women, as well as men, kept diaries during the Colonial period. Some of these consist of such bare notes of daily occurrence that they scarcely deserve inclusion in the annals of literature. Others are composed in a more ample vein, and give well-rounded pictures of the times. Such are the account of life in Philadelphia in 1772, written by Sarah Eve to entertain her absent father; the description of a journey across Connecticut taken by Bethiah Baldwin in 1770 to attend her brother's ordination; and perhaps most interesting of all, the diary-letters to her mother written by Anna Green Winslow from Boston, in 1771 to 1774. Anna was only eleven to thirteen years old at this time, and she was living with her aunt, while she gained the benefit of a Boston education. Her faithful reports to her mother of all she was doing, and the news among her mother's friends and relatives, give a vivid and entertaining picture of domestic life just before the Revolution. After reading the pages of this naïve, yet discerning little school-girl, one is saddened to learn that she died only a few years later, in 1779.

Many tempting bits might be quoted from Anna's diary, but one must suffice: [1]

. . . I hope Aunt won't let me wear the black Hatt with the red Dominie — for the people will ask what

---

[1] Winslow, p. 7.

COLONIAL WOMEN OF AFFAIRS

I have got to sell as I go along street if I do, or, how the folk at New guinie do? Dear mama, you don't know the fation here — I beg to look like other folk. You don't know what a stir would be made in sudbury street, were I to make my appearance there in my red Dominie and black Hatt.

A very human little school-girl, after all!

A group of women made their appearance at about the time of the Revolution, who wrote not only entertaining letters, but also verse, with very tolerable ease, if not with real inspiration. Among these women may be mentioned Mercy Warren, Abigail Adams, Elizabeth Fergusson, Susannah Wright, Hannah Griffets, and Anne Stockton. As the greater part of their production was later than 1776, and as they have been dealt with at length in the many interesting accounts of women of the Revolutionary period, it is unnecessary to go into details about them here.[1]

One woman poet of the time, however, should not be unnoticed. Phillis Wheatley was born in Africa, somewhere about 1755; carried to Boston, a shivering, ragged little girl, she was sold as a slave in 1761. Fortunately her purchaser was a kind and cultivated woman, Mrs. John Wheatley. She gave the child an excellent education for the times, in-

[1] See Wharton, *Colonial Days and Dames.*

PHILLIS WHEATLEY

cluding even astronomy and Latin. Phillis made phenomenal progress, and soon began writing verse which received much applause. Always delicate, in 1773 she was advised to take a sea voyage, and went to England with a member of the Wheatley family who was going on business. In London she was received with marked honor; while there the first edition of her poems came out, dedicated to the Countess of Huntingdon, who in particular had befriended her. Her visit was cut short because of the serious illness of Mrs. Wheatley, who died not long after Phillis's return in 1774. Other members of the family died within the next year or two, and Phillis, now free, married a colored man named Peters. She had three children, none of whom survived infancy. Her friends of earlier days were scattered by death and the fortunes of war; her husband was too indolent to work, and her last days were passed in extreme poverty and suffering. She died December 5, 1784.[1]

The verses of Phillis Wheatley are largely conventional and imitative; but they are generally pleasing, and have touches of originality that give reasonable hope that, had her life been prolonged and more fortunate, she might have written genuine poetry. Her character was as attractive as her

[1] Wheatley, *Memoir.*

career was remarkable; under adulation she was modest, under suffering uncomplaining.

The following is the concluding stanza of her "Hymn to the Evening": [1]

> "Filled with the praise of Him who gives the light,
> And draws the sable curtains of the night,
> Let placid slumbers soothe each weary mind,
> At morn to wake, more heavenly, more refined;
> So shall the labors of the day begin
> More pure, more guarded from the snares of sin.
> Night's leaden sceptre seals my weary eyes,
> Then cease, my song, till fair Aurora rise."

B. Religious Leaders

The founders of New England had the best intentions in the world of obeying the injunctions of St. Paul, when he said: "Let the woman learn in silence with all subjection. But I suffer not a woman to teach, nor to usurp authority over the man, but to be in silence." (1 Tim. 2, 11–12.) Alas for the best-laid plans, even of Puritan fathers! The colony of Massachusetts Bay had been settled only seven years, when its ecclesiastical, and even its civil government, was nearly overthrown by a woman. This woman, Anne Marbury Hutchinson, was born in England about 1600, and is said to have been a cousin of the poet Dryden; she came to Boston with her husband in 1634. In 1637, Win-

[1] Wheatley, p. 75.

throp states that she was holding two meetings weekly at her house, "wherto sixty or eighty persons did usually resort." [1] At first, there had been only one meeting a week, chiefly attended by women, for whose benefit Mrs. Hutchinson reviewed the sermon of the preceding Sunday. Soon she added critical comments of her own, which were generally unfavorable to the ministers. It is probable that her influence among the women was based upon her kindness and her skill as a nurse; but the vigor of her intellect soon attracted to her side many men, indeed nearly all of the Boston church. It is impossible to understand altogether the theological differences which separated her from the bulk of the ministers, but each party was equally convinced of the depth of the intervening gulf. It is needless to go into details of the persecution which followed. At her trial, Mrs. Hutchinson defended herself with courage and ability; but the decision was a foregone conclusion, unless indeed she would wholly and ignominiously retract. This she refused to do. Consequently, although she was pregnant at the time, she was banished from the jurisdiction of Massachusetts. Her husband and some adherents who were also banished, joined with her in founding the town of

[1] Winthrop. vol. I, p. 294.

Portsmouth. This was the second settlement in Rhode Island — two years after Roger Williams had established a refuge for civil and religious liberty at Providence. From the little group at Portsmouth, at first numbering only eighteen, the town of Newport soon sprang. After the death of her husband, Mrs. Hutchinson with her younger children moved to Long Island Sound, near the present New Rochelle, where they were massacred by the Indians in 1643. It has been asserted that this last removal was due to Mrs. Hutchinson's inability to live in peace, even with those who had endured banishment for espousing her doctrines; but there does not seem to be sufficient foundation for this charge, which the bitterness of party feeling may easily have invented. A fear that the jurisdiction of Massachusetts might be extended over Rhode Island, as then appeared likely, is a reasonable explanation of her removal. It is painful to find a contemporary Massachusetts minister, the Reverend Thomas Welde, commenting on Mrs. Hutchinson's death thus: [1]

. . . God's hand is the more apparently seen herein, to pick out this woful woman, to make her, and those belonging to her, an unheard of heavy example of their [i.e., the Indians'] cruelty above others.

[1] Winthrop, vol. I, p. 310, and vol. II, p. 164, notes.

AN

ELEGIAC
POEM,

On the DEATH of that celebrated Divine, and eminent
Servant of JESUS CHRIST, the Reverend and
learned

George *Whitefield*,

Chaplain to the Right Honourable the Countess of
HUNTINGDON, &c. &c.

Who made his Exit from this transitory State,
to dwell in the celestial Realms of Bliss, on LORD's-Day,
30th of September, 1770, when he was seiz'd with a Fit of the
Asthma, at Newbury-Port, near BOSTON, NEW-ENGLAND.

In which is a Condolatory Address to His truly noble
Benefactress the worthy and pious Lady HUNTINGDON ;---
and the Orphan-Children in GEORGIA, who, with many
Thousands are left, by the Death of this great Man, to lament the Loss of a Father, Friend, and Benefactor.

By PHILLIS,

A Servant Girl, of 17 Years of Age, belonging to Mr.
J. WHEATLEY, of BOSTON :—She has been but 9
Years in this Country from AFRICA.

BOSTON:
Printed and Sold by EZEKIEL RUSSELL, in Queen-street,
And JOHN BOYLES, in Marlboro'-street.

Time brought its revenges, and the grandson of Welde married a great-granddaughter of this woman whom the elder Welde had called "the American Jezebel." Other descendants of Mrs. Hutchinson held many of the most important offices in the gift of the colony of Massachusetts, and one — Thomas Hutchinson — was the last royal governor, and perhaps the ablest historian whom colonial America produced.

It has been said that the theological grounds of controversy between Mrs. Hutchinson and the orthodox party are too subtle for this untheological age to comprehend. One or two points stand out, however; she was the champion of individual freedom as against ecclesiastical tyranny; and her gospel was somewhat milder than that of the prevailing stern Calvinism. In a day when women were not supposed to have any brains at all, she upheld her own views with such ability that she won over, not only most of the women and the laymen with whom she came in contact, including the Governor, Sir Harry Vane, but even the leading minister of the colony, the Reverend John Cotton. These two, it is true, later bowed before the storm. She spread unfeigned consternation through the ranks of the orthodox, who indeed would have been defeated by the strength of her party had it not been for the help of the outlying towns, whose inhabitants had not come in direct contact with Mrs. Hutchinson's dynamic personality. Overwhelmed in Massachusetts, Mrs. Hutchinson carried her convictions to Rhode Island, where her followers helped to build up that commonwealth of freedom which Roger Williams, another outcast from Massachusetts, had established. Anne Hutchinson might appropriately stand as the patron saint of the Woman's Party. Kindly and helpful in all domestic and neighborly relations, she proved that a woman could form convictions of her own, that she could express and defend them with skill and eloquence, and that, if need be, she could suffer for them.[1]

The society of Friends has always recognized the ministry of women, and given them an equal part with men in all church affairs. Apparently the first members of that sect to come to America were Mary Fisher and Ann Austin, in 1656. Mary Fisher in particular had had an interesting career as a missionary, having gone even as far afield as to the court of the Sultan, who it is said received her courteously. The fathers of Massachusetts were less tolerant, and, after five weeks' imprisonment, sent these women back to England.[2]

[1] Ellis; Adams, *Three Episodes; Encyc. Brit.*, vol. xiv, pp. 12, 13.
[2] *Encyc. Brit.*, vol. xi, pp. 223, 227.

WITH TONGUE AND PEN

After the establishment of West New Jersey and Pennsylvania (1675–80), women are recorded as conducting regular evangelical tours. Most of these women came from Great Britain, and some returned there after a few years' preaching. Such were Mary (Neale) Paisley and Catherine (Payton) Phillips, who traveled through North and South Carolina, Virginia, Maryland, and Pennsylvania, during the years 1753 to 1756.[1]

One woman, whose active life was spent in this country, has left an autobiography, published in the "Friends' Library," under the title, "A Life of that Faithful Servant of Christ, Jane (Fenn) Hoskens, a Minister of the Gospel, among the People called Quakers." She was born in London, 1694; when sixteen years old, during an illness, she was told in a vision: "If I restore thee, go to Pennsylvania." Quite naturally, her parents opposed her design, and it was not until she was twenty-five years old, in 1719, that she was able to carry it into effect. Her early experiences as a governess in this country have already been alluded to. It was while living with these employers, who were Quakers, that she became convinced of her mission. She was told in a vision,[1] "I have chosen thee a vessel from thy youth to serve me, and to preach the Gospel of

[1] *Friends' Library*, vol. IX, pp. 73–119.

147

Salvation to my people. . . ." She replied, "Lord, I am weak, and altogether incapable of such a task, I hope Thou wilt spare me from such a mortification; besides I have spoken much against women appearing in that manner." Her reluctance yielded at length, however, and she started out on what her editor described as a highly successful career as preacher and missionary. At one time she went with another woman preacher named Elizabeth Levis on a tour through the Southern States and the Barbados. In 1756, when past sixty years old, with another devoted Quakeress, Susannah Brown, she traveled through New England.[1]

Governor Benedict Arnold, who died in 1678, left a three-year-old gray horse, to be kept for twenty years, for "the use of the women of the public ministry of the Quakers," who desired to visit New England, New York, or Philadelphia, in the course of their labors. Evidently women ministers were numerous and respected among the Friends.[2]

The teaching of Methodism in this country goes back to the missionary tours of Whitefield and Wesley; but as far as known, no church was organized until 1766. This was in New York, and

[1] *Friends' Library*, vol. I, pp. 460–73.
[2] Weeden, vol. II, p. 544.

was under the direct inspiration of a woman — Mrs. Barbara Heck.

Mrs. Heck, whose maiden name was Ruckle, was born in County Limerick, Ireland, in 1734. A little settlement had been established there by about fifty German families, who had been driven out of the Palatinate by Turenne. They were converted to Methodism by Wesley in 1753. Two years later, a small group of these people sailed for New York, where they lived quietly for some years. In 1766, Mrs. Heck, who had maintained her intense religious convictions, happened to find her brother and some friends playing a game of cards. Overcome with horror, she seized the cards and threw them into the fire, meanwhile solemnly warning the players of their spiritual danger. She then hurried to the house of her cousin, Philip Embury, to whom she exclaimed, "Brother Embury, you must preach to us, or we shall all go to hell, and God will require our blood at your hands!" The less impetuous Embury replied, "How can I preach? for I have neither a house nor a congregation." Undeterred, Mrs. Heck told him to preach in his own house, and promised to gather a congregation. She collected four persons, and he preached to them at once. This was the origin of the first Methodist society in America. It grew so rapidly that in two years a church building was needed. When it was proposed by one of the men, Mrs. Heck said that she had already made it a subject of prayer, and had received assurance of the Lord's help in the undertaking. She offered an architectural plan which combined economy and utility. This was accepted, and the church was built in John Street, Embury doing much of the carpentering, and Mrs. Heck whitewashing the walls. In 1769 missionaries from England came to take charge of this chapel, and Embury and the Hecks moved to Salem, Washington County, New York, where they started another Methodist society. At the outbreak of the Revolution Mrs. Heck and her family went to Canada, establishing a church there. Thus she is entitled to rank as the founder of Methodism in both the United States and Canada. She died at her son's house near Augusta in Upper Canada in 1804, aged seventy years.[1]

Before the end of the colonial period, man-governed ecclesiastic circles were destined to be disturbed by another woman named Ann. The world of 1770 was less intent upon theological matters than that of 1637 had been; consequently the disturbance was much less severe, although

[1] Buckley, vol. I, pp. 17, 119, 126; Stevens, Part III; *Encyc. Brit.*, vol. XVIII, p. 294.

to modern eyes Ann Lee, Shaker, seems a more startling figure than Mrs. Hutchinson or any Quaker Ann.

Ann Lee was born in Toad Lane, Manchester, England, in 1736, the daughter of a blacksmith. She was totally illiterate, and was sent to work young, first in a cotton factory. She was always thoughtful, with a strong sense of human depravity; although opposed to marriage, she was persuaded by her family to marry a young blacksmith named Stanley — a name, however, which she appears never to have borne. She had three children, all of whom died in infancy. In 1758, she united with a small group called Shakers, among whom she speedily became a leader. For nine years she endured severe spiritual sufferings, receiving divine manifestations from time to time, which she told to the society. On one occasion, while imprisoned for Sabbath-breaking, she had a vision in which she learned that celibacy was the only cure for human sin. After this she was called by her followers "Mother in spiritual things," and she called herself "Ann the Word." Mother Ann and her followers cultivated assiduously the gifts which her biographer says were all known to the primitive church — singing, dancing, shaking, shouting, speaking with tongues, and prophesying; and he adds: "These gifts progressively increased until the time of the full establishment of the church in America." The British public did not fully appreciate the exercise of these gifts, and made Mother Ann suffer many things. Once she was examined by a committee of hostile clergymen, all skilled linguists; after she had talked to them steadily for four hours, however, in seventy-two different tongues, they advised the populace to let her alone.

In 1774, Mother Ann received a message to take a select band, and go to America. On the voyage over, the captain's hardness of heart was overcome; he had objected to their holding meetings on deck, but soon a storm arose and a hole appeared in the ship. As he was giving way to despair, Mother Ann told him that an angel had just revealed to her that the ship would be saved; as she spoke, an unusually large wave struck the plank in the ship which had become loosened, and thrust it back into place.

This little company purchased land in Watervliet, New York, where they established a community of believers. Owing to the Revolution, they were obliged to remain quiet, relatively speaking, for several years, but in 1780 revivals began which met with considerable success. Mother Ann herself died in 1784.

Asked on one occasion how she, a woman, could

be the head of the church, Mother Ann replied:
"In nature — the children must be subject to their
parents, and the woman subject to her husband,
who is the first, and when the man is gone, the
right of government does not belong to the children
but to the woman. So in the family of Christ."
The implication of this statement forms the basis
of Shaker theology, which regards Mother Ann as
the female manifestation of divinity, and founder
of the second Christian Church, just as Jesus was
the male manifestation of divinity, and founder of
the first Christian Church. The movement died
out in England, but still persists in this country. It has a particular social interest, as it has
furnished an example of successful communism.
Women have always been prominent in its coun-
cils, one Lucy Wright having been head of the sect
from 1787 until 1821. The number of believers
probably reached its maximum about 1887, with
something like four thousand — a number reduced
to about one thousand in 1908.[1]

C. Actresses

The arts are seldom a preoccupation with settlers in a new country; and the pioneers in New
England, and the Quakers in Pennsylvania, were

[1] Evans, pp. 120 ff.; *Encyc. Brit.*, vol. xxiv, p. 771.

antagonistic to the stage, which they considered corrupting, and at the best a culpable waste of time. It is not to be expected, then, that actors would make an early appearance in the New World. By the time they did appear, women were playing freely in England, and women seem from the first to have shared equally with men in the establishment of the American stage.

Miscellaneous forms of entertainment may well have furnished occasional diversion to our fore-fathers for many years before the newspapers came into existence, but it is difficult to find records. By the time the press was established, exhibitions of wild animals were advertised, with an enthusiasm and ingenuity which indicate that people were quite willing to be fooled long before the days of Barnum. The "Boston Gazette" for January 1, 1722, carried the following exciting announcement:

At the South End of Boston, at the House of Mrs. Adam's is to be seen the LION, where on a Sign is writ these Words,

THE LION KING OF BEASTS IS TO BE SEEN HERE.

He is not only the Largest and most Noble, but the Tamest and most Beautiful Creature of his Kind, that has been seen, he grows daily, and is the Wonder of all that see him: Constant Attendance is given to all

Persons who desire to satisfy themselves with the sight of him.

Boston was one of the last places to be invaded by the theatre, but its citizens had other innocent amusements besides seeing lions, as the following card indicates: [1]

This notifies the Public that the Wax Work shown in this Town formerly by Mrs. Briggs, and lately by Mrs. Brooks, but has been out of Town this eight or ten years, is now to be shown (with a considerable Addition of Images and Dress) by Mrs. Hiller, in Cambridge Street, leading to West Boston, at Six Pence a piece, Lawful Money, for Men and Women, and Four Pence for Children, where also young Gentlewomen are taught Wax-work, Filligree, Transparent, &c, &c, and boarded or half-boarded, as they see cause.

At an earlier date a Philadelphia paper was advertising a woman entertainer who laid claim to no mean degree of professional skill: [2]

By permission of his Excellency Sir William Keith, Bart., Governor of the Province of Pennsylvania &c., This is to give notice to all Gentlemen, Ladies and others, That there is newly arrived to this place the famous Performers of Roap-Dancing, which is performed to the Admiration of all the Beholders.

1st. By a little Boy of seven Years old, who Dances

[1] *Boston Evening Post*, April 22, 1751.
[2] *American Mercury*, April 30, 1724.

and Capers upon the Strait Roap, to the Wonder of all Spectators.

2dly, By a Woman, who Dances *Corant* and *Jigg* upon the Roap, which she performs as well as any Dancing Master does it on the Ground.

3dly, She Dances with Baskits upon her Feet, and Iron Fetters upon her Legs.

4thly, She walkes upon the Roap with a Wheel-Barrow before her.

5thly, You will see various Performances upon the Slack Roap.

6thly, You are entertained with the Comical Humour of your old Friend *Pickle Herring.*

The whole concluded with a Woman turning round in a swift Motion with 7 or 8 Swords Points at her Eyes, Mouth, and Breast, for a Quarter of an Hour together, to the Admiration of all that Behold the Performance.

There will likewise be several other diverting Performances on the Stage, too large here to mention.

The above Performances are to be seen at the *New Booth* on *Society Hill*, To begin on *Thursday* next, being the last day of *April*, and to continue *Acting*, the Term of *Twenty Days* and no longer.

The price upon the stage is *3 shillings;* in the Pit *2 Shillings*, and in the Gallery *1 Shilling* and *6 Pence*.

To begin exactly at *Seven* o Clock in the Evening.

Different historians have claimed the honor of being the first professional theatrical company in America for different troupes; that of earliest date thus named was one promoted by William Livingston, who had conducted a dancing school in New

156

Kent County, Virginia. In 1716 he contracted to build a theatre at Williamsburg, with Charles and Mary Stagg, who had been his dancing pupils, as actors. Charles Stagg died in 1735, when his wife undertook to support herself by holding dancing assemblies. These received the approbation of society, and she was able to charge a good fee for them. The author of "Colonial Virginia" claims that Mrs. Stagg was the first leading lady in America.[1]

A company of players was acting in Philadelphia in 1749; apparently this was formed of English actors, with perhaps some local additions. Nancy Gouge (George?) is mentioned as being with it in Philadelphia, and accompanying it to New York in 1751, where she had a benefit performance. Benefits were also advertised for Mrs. Taylor, for the Widow Osborn, and for Mrs. Davis, "to enable her to buy off her time." It was a good many years before theatrical criticisms appeared, or indeed any newspaper notice except the paid advertisements. Our knowledge of this company is slight, but it appears to have disbanded after its New York appearance of 1751, then reorganized in the following year, and as "The Virginia Company of Comedians" toured the South for some years. It is men-

[1] Stanard, p. 230 ff.

tioned at Norfolk as late as 1768. Mrs. Osborn was the star, playing both men's and women's parts. Mrs. Parker, Miss Yapp, Mrs. and Miss Douthwaite, are also named in the company.[1]

Whatever the success of these theatrical ventures, an era may be said to have commenced for the American stage with the presentation at Williamsburg, on September 5, 1752, of the "Merchant of Venice," by the Hallam company from London. This company, under the management of Lewis Hallam, whose wife was the leading lady, gave the greatest English plays of the time. During two years, in which they appeared in Williamsburg, New York, and Philadelphia, they presented twenty-four full plays and eleven shorter pieces. Mrs. Hallam usually took the leading female part; a Mrs. Beccely, who appears to have joined the company subsequent to its Williamsburg engagement, was a singing soubrette, who acted "Polly" in the "Beggar's Opera," and kindred parts; Mrs. Adcock — probably the Miss Palmer who played Nerissa at Williamsburg — took second parts; Mrs. Love, the wife of a New York teacher of music, who joined the company as a dancer, was advanced to regular acting parts; and Miss Hallam, Mrs. Rigby, and Mrs. Clarkson filled in.[2]

[1] Seilhamer, vol. I, p. 11, ff.   [2] *Ibid.*, p. 35 ff.

MRS. HALLAM IN THE CHARACTER OF MARIANNE
IN FIELDING'S MISER

"Oh, uncle-in-law, look here! I never saw any so elegant in all my life."
From an old print

In 1754 the Hallam company left for Jamaica. Owing to the death of Lewis Hallam there, it was four years before the company returned to continental America. Meanwhile Mrs. Hallam had married an actor named Douglass, who reorganized the company.[1] They appeared in New York in the autumn of 1758; in Philadelphia the next spring for a season of six months; played during 1760 and the winter of 1760–61, at Annapolis, upper Marlborough, and Williamsburg; at Newport in the summer of 1761, and at Providence in 1762.[2] So far as known, these last are the only theatrical engagements in New England before the Revolution. At this period, Mrs. Douglass was still playing the lead, although in Newport she shared it with Mrs. Morris, who had joined the company in 1760; Mrs. Love was playing more difficult parts than formerly, and Mrs. Harman, an actress of experience, added strength to the cast. Thus in Philadelphia in 1759, when presenting "a tragedy written originally by Shakespeare, call'd the Tragical History of King Lear and his Three Daughters," Mrs. Love played Goneril, Mrs. Harman, Regan, and Mrs. Douglass, Cordelia.[3]

The Douglass company were first known as the

[1] Seilhamer, p. 87 ff.   [2] *Boston Evening Post*, August 9, 1762.
[3] *Pennsylvania Gazette*, September 27, 1759.

"Comedians from London." Colonial sentiment
was ceasing to find anything from London attractive, however, and in 1766 the name was changed
to the American Company. In this same year
Douglass opened the Southwark Theatre in Philadelphia.[1] It would probably seem very barren to
the modern playgoer; but it marked a distinct advance. By this time Mrs. Douglass was no longer
young, and she gradually yielded most of the leading parts to Miss Cheer, who made her first appearance with the company at this time. Miss
Wainwright, a talented singer, joined the company
then also. The season in Philadelphia was so successful that it was protracted into July, 1767, and
then supplemented by a short engagement from
September to November of the same year.[2] It was
then that the Storer sisters, whose names were long
to be associated with the American stage, made
their début on this side of the water. It is sometimes difficult to tell which Miss Storer is referred
to, as all were successful actresses. They were
Ann, afterward Mrs. Hogg, several of whose descendants have won distinction on the stage;
Fanny, Mrs. Mechler; and Maria, a good singer as
well as actress, later known as Mrs. Henry.

A theatre-goer of the time has left some com-

[1] Seilhamer, vol. 1, p. 153 ff.   [2] *Ibid.*, p. 196 ff.

ments on the American company as it was at this
period; he tells us that Miss Cheer was an admirable performer; that Miss Wainwright was said to
have been a pupil of the celebrated Dr. Arne; that
Mrs. Douglass, a respectable, matronly dame,
made a very good Gertrude; that Mrs. Harman
bore away the palm as a duenna, and Miss Wainwright as a chambermaid; and that the Misses
Storer and Miss Hallam were valuable acquisi-
tions.[1]

One would like to know more about Miss Cheer.
Whether or not she was a great actress, she must
have been an industrious one. In two years, she
played forty-five different parts, including Portia,
Ophelia, Juliet, Imogene, Cordelia, and Lady
Macbeth.[2] In the "Pennsylvania Chronicle" of
August 28, 1768, this interesting announcement
appears:[3]

Miss Cheer's Marriage.

Last week was married in Maryland, the Right
Honorable Lord Rosehill to Miss Margaret Cheer, a
young lady much admired for her theatrical performances.

This was before the days when actresses were frequent additions to the peerage. Alas, our knowl-

[1] Graydon's *Memoirs*, quoted *ibid.*, pp. 202–03.
[2] *Ibid.*, p. 205. [3] *Ibid.*, p. 207.

edge of this early romance goes no further. Lord
Rosehill is known to have been in the colonies at
that time, but there is nothing to indicate that Miss
Cheer returned with him to England. She did not
leave the stage until the following year; and she
made an occasional appearance in New York as
late as 1775.

The New York papers advertised a concert held
by Mrs. Harman on June 13, 1768; Mrs. Harman
was assisted by Miss Hallam, Maria Storer, and
Miss Wainwright.[1] Soon after this Miss Wainwright retired, living quietly in Philadelphia for
some years. Miss Hallam became leading lady this
season, appearing as Juliet on May 8th.[2]

Miss Hallam, who is spoken of as Mrs. Douglass's niece, aroused an enthusiasm never approached by Mrs. Douglass or Miss Cheer. She
apparently possessed considerable beauty, and an
admirer, bursting into poetry, exclaimed,[3]

"Ye Gods! 'Tis Cytherea's face!"

The company played in Annapolis and Williamsburg in 1770–71, and again in 1771–72. A letter
signed Y. Z., which appeared in the "Maryland
Gazette" of September 6, 1770, went into raptures
over Miss Hallam's performance of Imogene:[4]

[1] Graydon's *Memoirs*, p. 248. [2] *Ibid.*, p. 248.
[3] *Ibid.*, p. 338. [4] *Ibid*, p. 278–79.

For the Benefit of the Poor.

Thursday, December 20, 1753.

At the New Theatre in *Naffau-Street*.

This Evening, will be prefented,

(Being the laft Time of performing till the Holidays,)

A COMEDY, called,

LOVE for LOVE:

Sir Sampfon Legend,	by Mr. Malone.
Valentine,	by Mr. Rigby.
Scandal,	by Mr. Bell.
Tattle,	by Mr. Singleton.
Ben (the Sailor,)	by Mr. Hallam.
Forefight,	by Mr. Clarkfon.
Jeremy,	by Mr. Miller.
Buckram,	by Mr. Adcock.
Angelica,	by Mrs. Hallam.
Mrs. Forefight,	by Mrs. Rigby.
Mrs. Frail,	by Mrs. Adcock.
Mifs Prue,	by Mifs Hallam.
Nurfe,	by Mrs. Clarkfon.

End of Act 1*ft*, Singing by Mr. *Adcock*.

End of Act 2*d*, Singing by Mrs. *Love*.

In Act 3*d*, a Hornpipe by Mr *Hulett*.

End of Act 4*th*, a Cantata by Mrs. *Love*.

To which will be added, a Ballad Farce, called,

FLORA, or, Hob in the Well.

Hob,	by Mr. Hallam,
Friendly,	by Mr. Adcock.
Sir Thomas Tefly,	by Mr. Clarkfon.
Richard,	by Mafter L. Hallam.
Old Hob,	by Mr. Miller.
Flora,	by Mrs. Becceley.
Betty,	by Mifs Hallam.
Hob's Mother,	by Mrs. Clarkfon.

Prices : BOX, 6 s. PIT, 4 s. GALLERY, 2 s.

No Perfons whatever to be admitted behind the Scenes.

N.B. *Gentlemen and Ladies that chufe Tickets, may have them at Mr. Parker*

at Mr. —— Printing-Offices.

Money will —— taken at the Door.

The Company having been —— Pence being impos'd on us, at the Door of the
Houfe, we humbly —— —— form'd, that we are now forc'd to refufe taking
Pit 3 at the Door. To begin at 6 o'

AN OLD PLAYBILL

With the names of Mrs. Hallam, Miss Hallam, Mrs. Rigby, Mrs. Love,
Mrs. Becceley, and Mrs. Clarkson in the cast
See also the British coat of arms at the top

WITH TONGUE AND PEN

... She exceeded my utmost idea! Such delicacy of manner! Such classical strictness of expression! The music of her tongue — the vox liquida, how melting! ... methought I heard once more the warbling of Cibber in my ear.

The enthusiastic writer continued with pleasant comments on other members of the company:

The characteristical propriety of Mrs. Douglass cannot but be too striking to pass unnoticed. The fine genius of that young creature, Miss Storer, unquestionably affords the most pleasing prospect of an accomplished actress. The discerning part of an audience must cheerfully pay the tribute of applause due to the solid sense which is conspicuous in Mrs. Harman, as well as her perspicuity and strength of memory. . . . The merit of Mr. Douglas's company is notoriously in the opinion of every man of sense in America whose opportunities gives him a title to judge, — take them all in all — superior to those of any company in England, except those of the metropolis.

The Mrs. Morris who has been noted above, was drowned while crossing the ferry to New York, in December, 1767.[1] A second Mrs. Morris joined the company about 1770. Although said to have been without education, and to have a poor enunciation, she was long considered the principal attraction of the company. She is described as tall and elegant

[1] Graydon's *Memoirs*, p. 230.

in appearance, though rather affected, and with a mysterious manner which she cultivated even off the stage, never if possible allowing herself to be seen by the public in daylight. She played in Philadelphia until quite old, and died there in 1829.[1]

The approaching revolution interfered with the theatrical business, and the last season in the north before the war was that in New York from April to August, 1773. It is interesting that their farewell performance was "She Stoops to Conquer."[2] Rivington's Gazette for June 3, 1775, noted the death of Mrs. Catherine Maria Harman, the granddaughter of Colley Cibber, "a just actress and an exemplary woman." She left her property to Miss Cheer.[3]

The company made a visit to Charleston, South Carolina in 1774, and went from there to the West Indies.[4] They returned to the continent in 1785. Miss Hallam, however, is said to have established a fashionable boarding-school for girls in Virginia in 1775.[5]

A Mrs. Stamper, singer from the Theatre Royal, Edinburgh, was noted with the American company

[1] Graydon's *Memoirs*, p. 310 ff.
[2] *Ibid.*, p. 316. [3] *Ibid.*, p. 322, and Dunlap, p. 60.
[4] Dunlap, p. 63. [5] Stanard, p. 250.

in the season 1772–73.[1] It is said that the company never went to Boston, or, to quote an early writer:[2]

"At Boston they did not appear,
So peevish was the edict of the May'r."

But the "Boston Evening Post" for December 19, 1774, advertised:

For the benefit of Mrs. Stamper,
(who is in very distressed circumstances)
At Concert Hall,
On Thursday, the 29th instant, will be performed
A Concert of Vocal and Instrumental Musick;
which will be composed of the greatest Variety
of Instruments we have in Town.
To begin at Half after Six.
If the Ladies and Gentlemen chuse to dance after-
ward, there will be Ball-Musick provided.
Tickets to be had at the Bar of the British
Coffee House, at Col. Ingersol's, at Mr.
Ashby's, Watchmaker, and at the
Printer's, at Half a Dollar each.

The history of the colonial stage may perhaps appear meager; yet, when one considers all the circumstances of prejudice, relative poverty, and the pioneer nature of the undertaking, its record is remarkable. It is astonishing that any company should have had the courage to offer such difficult and extensive programmes year after year. The

[1] Seilhamer, p. 311.   [2] *Am. Antiq. Soc.*, 1921, p. 217.

company did not grow rich, but perhaps the fact that after all it received enough support to continue is somewhat to the credit of the country.

D. Printers

Sir William Berkeley, Governor of Virginia, answered a question addressed to him in 1671 by the Lords Commissioners of Foreign Plantations thus: [1]

I thank God there are no free schools nor printing, and I hope we shall not have these hundred years; for learning has brought disobedience and heresy and sects into the world, and *printing* has divulged them.

As it is notorious that women have always been a favored agent of the evil one in stirring up trouble, and sufficiently active on their own account in divulging what ought to be kept secret, Sir William would doubtless have had a satisfactory explanation for a phenomenon which might puzzle others — to wit, why colonial women distinguished themselves in maintaining printing presses and publishing newspapers. Be the explanation what it may, however, no less than eleven women ran printing presses, and ten of this number published newspapers in America before 1776.

The first woman printer of whom we have

[1] Wroth, p. 1.

166

COLONIAL PRINTING-PRESS
Owned by the American Antiquarian Society,
Worcester, Mass.

knowledge was Dinah Nuthead, whose husband
William Nuthead, having been prevented from
working in Virginia, had established a press at St.
Mary's, Maryland, in 1686. At his death in 1695
his wife inherited the printing press as well as the
rest of his estate of six pounds and nine shillings in
money. The Government had but just moved to
Annapolis, and thither Mrs. Nuthead went, carrying the press. In May, 1696, she asked and received license to set up her press; but she and two
friends were obliged to give bond that the press
would be used for nothing but blanks for the Government business, except by special permission of
the Governor!

This bond, which is still extant, shows a curious
fact: Mrs. Nuthead signed with a mark. In those
days a printing press was a rare article, and one
must suppose that Mrs. Nuthead relied on finding a
journeyman printer who could run it for her. Unfortunately, our knowledge of her enterprise goes
no further; some later records regarding the settlement of estates and guardianship of her children
indicate that she lived some years, and was apparently well thought of in the community.[1]

One sister-in-law of Benjamin Franklin's has
already been mentioned as a business woman.

[1] Wroth, p. 3. ff.

COLONIAL WOMEN OF AFFAIRS

Another sister-in-law attained greater prominence
and holds an honored place among colonial printers
of either sex. It will be remembered that Benjamin was apprenticed to an older brother James, a
printer. James had some difficulties with the Boston
authorities, and consequently moved his press to
Newport, where he became printer to the colony of
Rhode Island. A few years before this, in 1723, he
had married Anne, the daughter of Samuel Smith
of Boston. Upon James's early death, in 1735, "the
Widow Anne Franklin" continued the business.
She supplied blanks for the public offices and
printed pamphlets. The Rhode Island Government was less careful than that of Maryland that
the printing press should not divulge error. In
1740 she printed an edition of the laws of Rhode
Island, containing 340 pages folio. At this time
she was aided by her two daughters, and later by
her son, who was younger. Isaiah Thomas says: [1]

Her daughters were correct and quick compositors
at case; they were instructed by their father whom
they assisted. A gentleman who was acquainted with
Anne Franklin and her family informed me that he
had often seen her daughters at work in the printing
house, and that they were sensible and amiable
women.

In 1758, Anne's son, also named James, started the

[1] Thomas, vol. I, p. 420.

first newspaper in Rhode Island, the "Newport Mercury." At his premature death in 1762, his mother, now an elderly woman, continued the paper. She herself died, however, in 1763.[1]

As one regards the roll of early printers, one is tempted to believe that it was a condition of membership in the craft that all male members should agree to leave widows competent to carry on the business. In 1740, Andrew Bradford, of the Bradford family which furnished many New York and Philadelphia printers, married, as his second wife, Cornelia Smith, of New York. He died in 1742, and the widow continued his business of printing and bookselling, and publishing the "American Weekly Mercury." For about a year she had one Isaiah Warner as partner, but from 1744 to 1752 she managed alone.[2] It is said of Mrs. Bradford, "she was remarkable for Beauty and talents, but not so much for the amenities which give to female charms their crowning grace." [3]

One of the most interesting figures among colonial printers was John Peter Zenger, who published the "New York Weekly Journal." In 1722 he married as his second wife Anna Catherina Maul, of New York.[4] He died in 1746, leaving a

[1] Thomas, vol. I, p. 270.   [2] *Ibid.*, vol. II, p. 32.
[3] Jones, p. 27.   [4] Hildeburn, p. 7.

widow and six children, and in the issue of October 13 of that year the following card appeared in the "Journal":

The widow of the late Mr. John Peter Zenger, intending to continue Publishing the Paper, hopes that the Gentlemen who have been the Deceased's kind Benefactors will still continue to be such in encouraging the said Paper as before. They may still be supplied with all sorts of Blanks of any Kind, and all sorts of Printing-Work done reasonable and in the best Manner at the said Printing-Office in Stone-Street.

Apparently Mrs. Zenger had an unscrupulous competitor, for in the following year she addressed her patrons thus: [1]

This is to acquaint the Public that some Evil minded Persons have been pleased to spread a Report abroad that the Widow Zenger, Publisher of this Paper, had entirely dropped the Printing Business, &c. This is therefore to give Notice, that the said Report is Notoriously False, and that the said Widow still continues the Printing Business, where any Person may have their work done reasonable, in a good Manner, and with Expedition.

Several pamphlets printed by Mrs. Zenger are in existence. In December, 1748, she resigned the printing business to her step-son, John Zenger, but

[1] *New York Journal*, September 14, 1747.

she maintained a sort of stationery store for some time longer.[1]

Two distinguished women printers came to the work in aid of their son and brother. When William Goddard (born 1740) established the first printing press and the first newspaper in Providence, in June, 1762, his mother, Sarah Updike Goddard, lent him three hundred pounds for the enterprise. The paper, the "Providence Gazette," was well edited, but it did not receive very hearty support, and in 1765 it was discontinued. The following year, however, after the repeal of the Stamp Act, and while William was busy in New York, it was resumed by Sarah Goddard. She continued it successfully until November, 1768, when she sold out to John Carter, whom her son had sent from Philadelphia, where he then was, to help her. She joined her son in Philadelphia, and again invested in his business. She died there, Jan. 5, 1770.[2] The "New York Gazette" closed a sketch of her life thus:

Her conduct through all the changing trying scenes of life, was not only unblamable but exemplary; a sincere piety and unaffected humility, an easy agreeable cheerfulness and affability, an entertaining, sensible, and edifying conversation, and a prudent

---

[1] Thomas, vol. II, p. 101.
[2] Wroth, pp. 120–21. Thomas, vol. II, p. 272.

attention to all the duties of domestic life, endeared her to all of her acquaintances, especially in the relations of wife, parent, friend, and neighbor. The death of such a person is a public loss.

Mrs. Goddard's grandson, William Giles Goddard, became the editor of the "Rhode Island American," and professor of philosophy at Brown University.[1]
William Goddard was a restless person, and in February, 1774, he left Annapolis, where he was then editing the "Maryland Gazette," in order to work on the establishment of the postal system. His sister, Mary Katherine Goddard, took over the paper, at first temporarily. As he did not return, in the following year she dropped his name and assumed full responsibility. She conducted it with success throughout the trying years of the war. The paper sometimes had to be reduced in size, but it appeared, approximately on time, "a journal second to none in the colonies in interest." In her issue of November 16, 1779, she announced with truth, that her paper circulated as extensively as any on the continent. Isaiah Thomas says that she was "an expert and correct compositor of types." In addition to her editorial work, she was for many years the postmistress of Annapolis, at a time when postal revenues were very uncertain; at

[1] Opdyke, p. 93.

times she paid the riders "hard money," as she described it, from her own purse. Furthermore, she did good job printing, and kept a bookstore. In 1784, when the war was over, and the paper running well, her brother returned, and she relinquished it to him. The position as postmistress she held until 1789, and after that simply kept the bookstore. She died in 1814, aged about seventy-nine, and left a small property to a colored woman who had been her servant.[1]

The earliest date for the establishment of a printing press in South Carolina which can be proved is 1731; yet that State has the distinction of having had the first woman editor of a newspaper. Louis Timothee had been associated with Benjamin Franklin in Philadelphia; in 1734 he brought out the "South Carolina Gazette," at the same time anglicizing his name to Lewis Timothy. He was accidentally killed in December, 1738. The next number of the paper appeared on time, however, published by his widow Elizabeth, with the aid of her son Peter. She continued to publish it (for six or seven years, according to one authority, and for two years only, according to another) until she sold it to her son. It is interesting to note that this son Peter's widow in due time continued the

[1] Wroth, pp. 144-45.

paper, until she in turn sold it to her son, Benjamin Franklin Timothy.[1]

Dinah Nuthead and Ann Franklin both antedated Elizabeth Timothy as printers, but Mrs. Nuthead had no connection with a newspaper, and the "Newport Mercury" was not started until 1758; consequently it appears that Mrs. Timothy deserves to be called the pioneer woman journalist. Several other women have been printers and publishers in South Carolina; according to Heartman, Mrs. Mary Crouch maintained a press in Charleston from 1775 to 1780;[2] other authority gives 1778 as the date when she commenced printing.[3]

The Green family of Massachusetts holds a high, perhaps the highest, place in the history of early printing in America. Jonas Green left the family home, and started south. In Philadelphia in 1738 he married Ann Catharine Hoof, a Dutchwoman by birth; they had a family of fourteen children, only six of whom reached maturity.

Jonas Green did not stay long in Philadelphia; going still farther south, he established a business at Annapolis, which the historian of Maryland calls "the most famous of Maryland presses." He

[1] Salley, pp. 33-35.   [2] Heartman, *Checklist*, p. 17.
[3] Salley, p. 65.

not only published the "Annapolis Gazette," but also did all the government printing until his death, in April, 1767. The newspaper which contains the notice of his death contains also the following:

I presume to address you for your countenance to myself and numerous Family, left, without your Favour, almost destitute of Support by the Decease of my Husband, who long, and I have the Satisfaction to say, faithfully served you in the Business of Provincial Printer; and, I flatter myself, that with your kind Indulgence and Encouragement, Myself and Son will be enabled to continue it on the same Footing.

To quote again from the Maryland historian, "Under her management neither the Gazette nor the public printing suffered retrenchment or deterioration." She completed the "Acts and Votes" for 1767; in the following year the Assembly testified their satisfaction with her work, and voted her in payment the sum of "nine hundred and forty-eight dollars and one half dollar"; and thereafter 48,000 pounds of tobacco annually for years when the assembly was in session, and 36,109 pounds for other years. During the eight years that she continued as public printer, this rate of pay was unchanged. Besides the public work, she printed almanacs, some political pamphlets, and satirical pieces. "The Charter and Bye-Laws of the City of

Annapolis" from her press is one of the best pieces of colonial printing extant.

The business of publishing a paper had its hazards. At one time a heated political controversy was waged in the columns of her paper; one of the disputants was well known, but his opponent, who was particularly scurrilous, hid his identity under the signature of the "Bystander." At length Mrs. Green refused to print anything more from him, unless he would reveal his name, and would guarantee her against suit for slander. As the man in question considered this a rank bit of favoritism, he did not comply, but threatened to knock up her press if ever she printed anything from the other side.

The "Maryland Gazette" for March 30, 1775, contains a notice of Mrs. Green's death and this tribute to her character: "She was of a mild and benevolent disposition, and for Conjugal Affection, and Parental Tenderness, an Example to her Sex." Her three sons, and several grandsons, became distinguished printers.[1]

Another Southern paper, the "Virginia Gazette," was published at one time by a woman; Clementina Rind continued it after the death of her husband in August, 1773, until her own death two years later.[2]

[1] Wroth, pp. 76–84, 90 ff.   [2] *Ibid.*, p. 87.

WITH TONGUE AND PEN

The earliest paper in the American colonies was the "Boston Newsletter." Upon the death of its editor, Richard Draper, in June, 1774, it was continued by his widow, Margaret Draper. Beside publishing the paper, she was printer for the Governor and Council. Shortly after the outbreak of the Revolutionary War, when Boston was besieged, all the other newspapers ceased publication. As the Drapers were loyalists, Mrs. Draper continued until the British left Boston. Hence the "Newsletter" has the distinction of being not only the first paper, but also the last paper, in colonial Boston. At the British evacuation, Mrs. Draper went to Halifax, and thence to England, where she died a few years later.[1]

Modern newspaper editors assure the public from time to time in plaintive language that theirs is no easy task. Whatever the case may be now, an editorial chair must have been a very uncomfortable place in colonial days. To be sure, the papers appeared once a week instead of daily; but one has only to look at a colonial printing press, and then compare it with modern machinery, to be convinced that the advantage is all with the present day. Originally the editor was also compositor, printer, news writer, city editor, society editor,

[1] Thomas, vol. I, p. 393.

177

and everything else. In addition he ran a lost and found office, an employment agency, and probably a general store. To judge by the advertisements, everything, from a wet-nurse to lamp-black, might be obtained if one would "enquire of the printer." It does not appear that printers were in the habit of amassing a fortune, either. Their failure to do so may be one reason why their widows so promptly determined to continue the business. It is said that Andrew Bradford left his widow well provided. The inventory of William Nuthead's estate proves that his widow was less fortunate; and the language with which other widows address the public indicates that most of them were under the necessity of supporting their families. The small returns might well have moved these widows to seek other means of support; but the printing business represented a considerable outlay of capital, and an accumulated good-will, which could not always find a ready market. In some instances, the widow may have carried on the business only until she could find a purchaser. In other cases, there was a son growing up who would be glad to have a business ready for him in a few years. Undoubtedly family pride in achievement played its part. Another reason was probably equally important in inducing these widows to carry on the family press; in

THE
DEPUTY COMMISSARY'S
GUIDE

Within the Province

—— OF ——

—— together ——

With plain and sufficient directions for Testators to form, and Executors to perform their Wills and Testaments; for administrators to compleat their Administrations, and for every Person any way concerned in deceased Person's Estates, to proceed therein with Safety to themselves and others.

by ELIE VALLETTE.

Register of the Prerogative Office *of the Said Province.*

ANNAPOLIS,

Printed by *Ann Catharine Green* and Son.

MDCCLXXIV.   *J. Sparrow Sculp*.

ENGRAVED TITLE OF A BOOK PRINTED BY
ANN CATHARINE GREEN AND SON

those days, when enterprises were on a small scale, and were usually maintained in the house of the owner, undoubtedly the women of the family frequently helped in the various processes of printing, and in effect served as apprentices. Consequently they became skilled workmen, and could more easily carry on the same business than undertake anything else, although other lines were certainly easier, and at least equally remunerative. In spite of all explanations, however, the fact remains remarkable that so many of the most important colonial newspapers should have been published, and successfully published, by women.

CONCLUSION

THE attempt to visualize the work of women in colonial times is somewhat like watching a play by occasional flashes of lightning. The information available is provokingly casual, and it is a temptation to let one's imagination range in filling up the gaps. Town records, court records, tax lists, wills and family papers, all of which have been consulted, contain a mine of information which it would take a lifetime to master. Yet when this is done, it is probable that some of the gaps will still remain.

The present study makes no claim to being exhaustive; it has done little more than scratch the surface — although scratching the surface has not been an altogether easy task. A huge mass of material has often yielded only a tiny nugget of what, from the author's standpoint, was precious metal. Yet it has been a source of great encouragement that scarcely a file of newspapers, a diary, or other whole work has been read which did not yield some evidence of woman's activity.

Daily work was a matter of course to our ancestors, and nothing to call for much comment, whether in formal history or private diary. Some

CONCLUSION

lines of effort attracted more attention than others. It is probable that the greater part of the authors, actresses, printers, and religious leaders, except among the Friends, have been discovered; and of those found, most have been mentioned in these pages. The same is by no means true of women in any of the other occupations noted — innkeepers, shopkeepers, craftswomen, nurses, teachers, or still less, landowners. Only a fraction of those found have been named here; and there is every reason to suppose that the total numbers were much greater than those found — in some instances doubtless many times as great. Consequently it would be futile from the material in hand to attempt any statistical conclusion, or even comparisons. Yet some facts stand out.

It should be remembered that most women in the colonial era had husbands to support them. Marriages were early, nearly every one did marry, and in case of widowhood remarriage was frequent. According to the census of 1900, on the other hand, more than one quarter of the total female population, sixteen years and over, was unmarried, and from this quarter came about two thirds of the female bread-winners; the other third was formed of the married, widowed, and divorced, combined.[1]

[1] *Women at Work*, pp. 13 and 15.

COLONIAL WOMEN OF AFFAIRS

Again, the woman's part of the family work was more pressing before the days of apartment houses and vacuum cleaners. Few colonial women turned to outside work because time hung heavy on their hands.

On the other hand, everything indicates that, should need arise, there was nothing in the social or economic code of the times to prevent a woman's supporting herself and her family in whatever way she best could. In a new country, there was plenty of work to be done, and the accumulation of capital either in families or in the community which could be devoted to charitable purposes was limited. Furthermore, the Puritan religion abhorred idleness. For these reasons, the single woman, the wife with incapacitated or deserting husband, or the widow, were encouraged to work. Under the system of domestic industries then in vogue, it was common for a woman to help her husband in his work, and there were no social prejudices to prevent her carrying on the business if he died. Neither was she debarred from continuing it if she remarried. Indeed, it appears that there was no objection to a married woman's supplementing the family income by any means she found convenient. Numerous married women have been noted among the teachers — a contrast

CONCLUSION

to modern conditions, in which it is doubtful whether change has been altogether on the side of progress.

Different kinds of work varied less in their social standing in colonial times than they do to-day. This was largely due to the homogeneity of society. As far as the white population was concerned, those who had been brought over as servants soon acquired land, and made their place in the community according to their abilities. It appears to have been allowable in New England for young girls of the leading families to go out to service. Sewall notes in his diary that his eighteen-year-old sister Jane, from Newbury, was planning to go as maid with a Boston family.[1]

Even as late as the period of the revolution, there are evidences of a democratic attitude toward work. The attractive advertisements of groceries, offered by Mrs. Sheaffe, which were quoted in Chapter II, may be recalled. Mrs. Susannah Sheaffe was the daughter of Thomas Child, one of the founders of Trinity Church, Boston, and was the widow of William Sheaffe, deputy collector of customs. At his death in 1771, Mrs. Sheaffe was almost penniless, and her friends helped establish her in the grocery business.[2] As

[1] Sewall, vol. i., p. 34.   [2] Earle, *Colonial Dames*, p. 87.

she advertised frequently until the Revolution, it may be supposed that she was reasonably success-ful. Her large family of children grew up to occupy prominent positions, some on the British and others on the American side. One son became Sir Roger Hale Sheaffe; a daughter, Susannah, mar-ried an English captain; another became the wife of James Lovell, the famous Boston schoolmaster, orator, and patriot; a third daughter married a nephew of Governor Shirley; a fourth married Benjamin Cutler, high sheriff of Boston. Margaret Sheaffe, who became Mrs. John R. Livingston, was a celebrated beauty, and was distinguished by the friendship of Lafayette.[1]

This attitude was not confined to New England. Mrs. Alexander's business activities did not affect her position as a social leader in New York City, and we are told that for a long time she was the only person beside the Governor who drove a two-horse coach.[2]

The variety of occupations, and the number of women engaged in them, appear to increase as one approaches 1776; how far this was the fact, how-ever, is open to question. It must be borne in mind that the records for the later period are much more abundant. Probably the greater complexity of

[1] Earle, *Colonial Dames*, p. 87.   [2] Van Rensselaer, p. 236.

CONCLUSION

society brought greater specialization in work, which would attract more women; certainly some activities entirely new to the western hemisphere came into existence — as, for instance, acting. Furthermore, the increase in population would augment the absolute number of women at work. On the other hand, certain tendencies opposed to women's participation in industrial life, which will be discussed later, probably began to affect the larger cities at least before 1776.

This study has shown colonial women carrying on work, apparently in a legal and social atmosphere of almost entire freedom. Women's activity in church matters, or in literature, was certainly questioned, and medical careers were kept within definite limits. At first women had even a legal monopoly as midwives, and no objection to them in that capacity appeared until the nineteenth century. As far as general business went, women were to be found buying and selling, suing and being sued, acting as administrators and executors, and having power of attorney, with what appears to be the utmost freedom. The widow was commonly executor for her husband, a daughter frequently acted for her father, and women with less claim were sometimes chosen. The story has already been told how Governor Leonard Calvert of

COLONIAL WOMEN OF AFFAIRS

Maryland, dying in 1647, left Margaret Brent as his sole executor.

Perhaps no other colonial woman held quite such important legal responsibilities as Margaret Brent, but many others showed a capacity for affairs. In the "Providence Gazette" for August 8, 1768, Sarah Jenckes gave warning that as executor for her husband, Nathan Jenckes, Collector of Rates and Taxes, who had died before finishing collection, she would sue any who did not pay his taxes promptly, or give security satisfactory to her.

Colonial husbands appear to have been rather quick to advertise their refusal to pay future debts of their wives' contracting, sometimes because said wife had "eloped from me the subscriber without just cause," sometimes merely because of a suspected inclination to run into debt. Such husbands did not always go unchallenged, however. For instance, the "Boston Evening Post" contained the following dignified remonstrance:

WESTON, *July* 1, 1762

MESSRS. FLEET,

I find in your last Monday's Paper, that my Husband has informed the Publick, That I have eloped — and that I run him into Debt, and has given a Caution not to Trust me on his Account. Although I am

CONCLUSION

very sensible that neither he nor I are of much Importance to the Publick, for he has not an Estate to entitle me to any Credit on his account; yet I desire you to be so kind to me, as to let the Publick know, That I never run him in Debt in my Life, nor ever eloped, unless it was to Day Labour, to support me and the Children, which I am of Necessity obliged to do; and shall be ever glad to do my Duty to him, and wish he would for the future behave to me in such a Manner that I may do it with more Ease than heretofore.

her
Mary X Willington
Mark

The ungallant husband, Josiah, had signed his communication with a mark also. The town records of Weston support Mrs. Willington's statement about her husband's property; in 1757 he was assessed at eight pence for personal property, and three pounds for real estate. The records give also the births of seven children, born between 1733 and 1751.[1]

Some husbands did not escape as easily as Josiah Willington. On July 31, 1746, one John Fenbey, porter, posted his wife Mary in the "Pennsylvania Gazette." Her reply came promptly:[2]

Whereas John, the Husband of Mary Fenbey, hath

---

[1] Weston *Tax Lists*, p. 2; *Vital Records*, pp. 46, 57, 58.
[2] *Pennsylvania Gazette*, August 7, 1746.

advertised her in this Paper as *eloped* from him, &c, tho' 'tis well known they parted by Consent, and agreed to divide their Goods in a Manner which he has not yet been so just as fully to comply with, but detains Her Bed and Wedding Ring: And as she neither has, nor desires to run him into Debt, believing her own Credit to be fully as good as his; so she desires no one would trust him on her Account, for neither will she pay any Debts of his contracting.

MARY FENBEY

There is not much evidence of women's exerting direct political influence in colonial times. The letter from the widows of New York, quoted in Chapter II, indicates that some of them already aspired to civic responsibility. In some places this was not wholly confined to aspiration. The list of voters for the March meeting, 1775, in Worcester, Massachusetts, "Qualified according to the Last List of Estates by which the Taxes are made," contained 193 names, among which are to be found those of Sarah Chandler, Mary Stearns, and Mary Walker.[1]

A curious case of a woman's exercising political influence is recorded in Thompson's "History of Long Island." In 1654, Governor Stuyvesant refused to confirm the election of two magistrates of Gravesend, although they were men of importance

[1] *Worcester*, p. 118.

CONCLUSION

there. His action aroused so much excitement that he felt it advisable to go to Gravesend in person, to appease the discontent. In order to achieve his object, he found it necessary to enlist the good offices of Lady Deborah Moody, one of the original patentees of the town. He allowed her to nominate the magistrates for that year, and her popularity reconciled the people to this unusual measure.[1]

The idea has been current that the women of colonial days suffered from severe legal and social handicaps, if they made any attempt to go outside the limited home circle. Handicaps, according to present notions, may well have existed; but the evidence here presented indicates that they did not interfere with women's activity in a large variety of undertakings. Most of the discussions, such as were frequent a few years ago when the question of "women's rights" was acute, really take little cognizance of the colonial period. A few references to days before 1776 are generally to be found, but the greater part of the argument is based on conditions in the early and middle parts of the nineteenth century. Is it possible that conditions were worse then than they had been in the previous century? This cannot be determined without a thorough analysis of the laws and customs of the

[1] Thompson (ed. 1839), pp. 83–84.

colonial period — such as this study does not attempt. Some reasons may be given, however,
which might explain such a change, but they are
nothing more than hypotheses.

First, in the early days there were few codes,
legal or traditional; matters were dealt with as they
came up — according to English common law, to
be sure, but the common law adapted to fit new
conditions. After the Revolution there developed a
mania for codifying, and of course this codification
was all done by men. It may be that men were not
then ready to admit in words some conditions which
in the exigencies of previous times had been tacitly
permitted; and so, perhaps unconsciously, they curtailed the existing privileges of women.

Second, on the whole the country had been
getting wealthier; although the process was interrupted by the Revolution, it was accelerated after
the War of 1812. Commercial prosperity, and the
beginnings of industrialization hastened the natural
growth of prosperity. It seems to be a law of life
that as people become prosperous they desire to
multiply their luxuries, and it has been demon-
strated repeatedly that of all luxuries one of the
most coveted is the possession of "ladies," a class
of women, that is, who reflect credit upon their
husbands and fathers in exact proportion to their

CONCLUSION

uselessness.[1] Under pioneer conditions, a lady — using the word in this restricted sense — is as much out of place as a prize Pomeranian would be. Every one had to row his or her own weight. Consequently when the descendants of pioneers wish to prove the extent of their progress from small beginnings, no more attractive way presents itself than by acquiring a useless and ornamental womankind. This common tendency was accentuated in America by the immigration which followed the Industrial Revolution here. The presence of a large group whose women worked at menial occupations, and who were socially objectionable to the older settlers from every point of view, increased the desirability of keeping their own women sheltered. In discussing woman's place in Roman society, Mrs. Putnam says: "It would have been as difficult to find the lady in early Italy as in early Massachusetts." This implication as to Massachusetts is borne out by the facts here presented. The situation was quite different in the days when our mothers and grandmothers were young.

A third possible cause of change is to be found in the different working conditions which the Industrial Revolution brought about. Previously, fac-

[1] For discussion of this theory see Veblen, pp. 54–57; 178–80; 352–53; and especially Putnam, "The Lady."

tories and shops were located in the house of the proprietor, or at any rate in an adjoining building; it was easy and natural to enlist the aid of his family, and as the enterprises were generally small, this was often sufficient. In this way a great many women received real vocational training, and practical business experience. The condition was changed when business was conducted on a larger scale, in a building frequently at a distance from the house, and with the aid of many employees. The mother or daughter could less easily combine some assistance in the shop with her domestic duties; and the presence of employees, who soon began to come from a racially different group, made such assistance undesired.

Still another reason, affecting certain lines of work, may be found in the growing recognition of the need for academic preparation to supplant the apprenticeship method. It has been shown how women might almost imperceptibly acquire experience; it was not possible to acquire a formal professional education imperceptibly, and men were not yet willing to admit women to higher education. This attitude is obvious in the words of the Boston physician, quoted in Chapter IV. The objection was less to women's practicing as midwives, than to their being trained in midwifery.

CONCLUSION

The foregoing is after all merely speculation. The achievements of the women here chronicled rest on a more substantial foundation, and justify at least one conclusion. These women were no more all the stereotyped pilgrim mother of painting and sculpture, or the colonial dame of fancy dress ball, than we of to-day are all missionary heroines or fashion-plate models. They were of all kinds, and very human. Some of them did not pay their debts, some overcharged, some became bankrupt, some broke their agreements, and one, we are told, was insufficiently supplied with those "amenities which give to female charms their crowning grace." A perusal of the court records would suggest many other, and more offensive, faults which might be laid to their account. But most of these women, and many others like them, showed courage and devotion which are beyond praise.

Women nowadays are prone to blazon the achievements of their sex. The method of their foremothers was different. In trying to find out what they really did accomplish, one wishes that they had been less unassuming. But they did what they were called upon to do, of whatever nature, and for the most part they did it uncomplainingly and well. It is pleasant to know (and it takes away some part of the familiar jibe about their having to endure the forefathers) that on the whole the men of the time accorded them honor. No finer epitaph has ever been written than that by big-hearted Judge Sewall, about one who was probably a very simple woman:

July 24, 1715. Mrs. Anne Kay was buried. — Aged 74, was born at Manchester. Was a good woman, and a good school-mistress.

THE END

REFERENCES

REFERENCES

ABBOT, EDITH. *Women in Industry; a Study in American Economic History.* New York, 1910.

ADAMS, C. F. *Three Episodes of Massachusetts History.* 2 vols. Boston, 1892.

AMERICAN ANTIQUARIAN SOCIETY. *Proceedings.* 1921.

American Weekly Mercury. Philadelphia, 1719 ff.

Ames, Dr. Nathaniel, Extracts from the Diary of. Dedham *Historical Register,* vol. 1 ff.

ARMSTRONG, ZELLA. *Notable Southern Families.* 2 vols. Chattanooga, 1918.

BALDWIN, BETHIA. *A Ride across Connecticut before the Revolution* (1770); S. E. Baldwin, ed., New Haven Historical Society Papers, vol. IX.

BARTLETT, JOSIAH, M.D. *A Dissertation on the Progress of Medical Science in the Commonwealth of Massachusetts.* Boston, 1810.

Boston Evening Post. 1735 ff.

Boston Gazette. 1755 ff.

Boston Newsletter. 1704 ff.

Boston Marriages. 1700–1751.

Boston, Memorial History of. Boston, 1880.

BRADFORD, WILLIAM. *History of Plymouth Plantation, 1606–1646.* W. T. Davis, ed. New York, 1920.

BRADSTREET, MRS. ANNE. *Poems, with her Prose Remains.* Introduction by C. E. Norton. New York, 1897.

BROWNE, WILLIAM HAND. *Maryland; A History of a Palatinate.* Boston, 1904.

BROOKS, GERALDINE. *Dames and Daughters of Colonial Days.* New York, 1900.

BRUCE, PHILIP ALEXANDER. *Economic History of Virginia in the Seventeenth Century.* New York, 1896.

REFERENCES

BUCKLEY, JAMES MONROE. *History of Methodism in the United States.* 2 vols. New York, 1897.

Bumstead, Jeremiah, Diary of. New England Register. July and October, 1861.

CALHOUN, ARTHUR W. *Social History of the American Family.* Vol. 1, Colonial Period. Cleveland, 1917.

Cambridge, Massachusetts, History of, 1630–1877. L. R. Paige. Boston, 1877.

Camden County, New Jersey, History of. G. R. Prowell. Philadelphia, 1886.

CROCKER, HANNAH MATHER. *Observations on the Real Rights of Women.* Boston, 1818.

Dictionary of National Biography. New York, 1908.

Dorchester, Massachusetts, History of the Town of. Boston, 1859.

DUNLAP, W. *History of the American Theatre.* Vol. 1. London, 1833.

EARLE, ALICE MORSE. *Colonial Dames and Goodwives.* Boston, 1895.

EARLE, ALICE MORSE. *Stage-Coach and Tavern Days.* New York, 1900.

EARLE, ALICE MORSE. *Margaret Winthrop.* New York, 1895.

ELLET, ELIZABETH F. *Women of the American Revolution.* 3 vols. 4th ed. New York, 1849.

ELLIS, GEORGE E. *Life of Anne Hutchinson,* in *Library of American Biography* (Sparkes), vol. 16. Boston, 1847.

Encyclopædia Britannica. 11th edition.

ESSEX COURTS. *Quarterly Records of Essex County Courts,* vols. I–III, 1639–1671. Salem, 1911 ff.

Essex County Gazette. 1768 ff.

EVANS, F. W. *Ann Lee, the Founder of the Shakers.* 4th ed. London, 1858.

Eve, Sarah, Diary of, 1772. Pennsylvania Magazine of History and Biography, vol. 5.

REFERENCES

Fleming, William and Elizabeth, Narrative of the Sufferings and Surprising Delivery of. Boston, 1756.

FOSDICK, L. J. *French Blood in America.* N.Y., 1906.

Friends' Library, vols. I–IX. Philadelphia, 1837–1847.

Holyoke Diaries, 1709–1856. G. F. Dow, ed. Salem, 1911.

Goelet, Capt. Francis, Extracts from the Diary of, 1746–1750. New England Register, vol. 24.

GRANT, MRS. ANNE. *Memoirs of an American Lady.* Albany, 1876.

HEARTMANN, FRED. *Checklist of Printers in the United States till 1783.* New York, 1915.

HILDEBURN, C. R. *Sketches of Printers and Printing in Colonial New York.* New York, 1895.

Hiltzheimer, Jacob, Extracts from the Diary of, 1765–1798. J. C. Parsons, ed. Philadelphia, 1895.

HUMPHREYS, MARY GAY. *Catherine Schuyler.* New York, 1897.

JONES, H. G. *Andrew Bradford, Founder of the Newspaper Press in the Middle States of America.* Philadelphia, 1869.

KNIGHT, MADAM SARAH. *The Private Journal of a Journey from Boston to New York in the Year 1704.* Albany, 1865.

Lancaster County, Pennsylvania, History of. Ellis and Evans. Philadelphia, 1883.

Lexington, History of the Town of. Hudson. Boston, 1913.

LLOYD, MARY. *Meditations on Divine Subjects.* New York, 1751.

MAINE HISTORICAL SOCIETY. *Collections,* vol. I.

MASON, GEORGE. *Reminiscences of Newport.* Newport, 1884.

Mass. Colonial Records, vol. II, 1642–49. Boston, 1853.

MEYER, ANNIE NATHAN, editor. *Woman's Work in America.* New York, 1891.

New York Gazette and Weekly Postboy. 1746 ff.

New York Mercury. 1752 ff.

New York Weekly Journal. 1733 ff.

REFERENCES

New York Tax Lists, 1695–99.

NORCROSS, F. W. "Ye Ancient Inns of Boston Town." *New England Magazine*, November, 1901.

OPDYKE, C. W. *Op Dyck Genealogy.* Albany, 1889.

Parkman, Rev. Ebenezer, Extracts from the Diary of. H. M. Forbes, ed. Worcester, 1899.

Pennsylvania Gazette. 1728 ff.

Pennsylvania Mercury, and Universal Advertiser. 1790.

PHYSICIAN. *Remarks on the Employment of Females as Practitioners in Midwifery.* By a Physician. Boston, 1828.

Providence Gazette, and County Journal. 1762 ff.

PUTNAM, EMILY JAMES. *The Lady; Studies of Certain Significant Phases of Her History.* New York, 1910.

RAVENEL, HARRIOTT HORRY. *Eliza Pinckney.* New York, 1896.

Rehoboth, History of. Leonard Bliss, Jr. Boston, 1836.

Rowlandson, Mrs. Mary, The Narrative of the Captivity and Restoration of (1682). Lancaster, 1903.

SALLEY, A. S., JR. *First Presses of South Carolina.* Bibliographical Society of America. *Proceedings and Papers,* vol. 2. 1907–08.

SCHAW, JANET. *Journal of a Lady of Quality* (Andrews, ed.). New Haven, 1922.

SEILHAMER, G. O. *History of the American Theatre.* New York, 1896.

Sewall Papers, 1673–1729. 3 vols. Massachusetts Historical Collections, 5th Series, vols. V–VII. Boston, 1878.

SLAFTER, CARLOS. "Schools and Teachers of Dedham." *Dedham Historical Register,* vol. 1 ff.

SMALL, WILLIAM HERBERT. *Early New England Schools.* Boston, 1914.

STANARD, MARY N. *Colonial Virginia; its People and Customs.* Philadelphia, 1917.

STEVENS, ABEL. *The Women of Methodism; its Three*

REFERENCES

Foundresses, Susanna Wesley, the Countess of Huntingdon, and Barbara Heck. New York, 1866.

THOMAS, ISAIAH. *History of Printing.* 2 vols. Worcester, 1810.

THOMPSON, BENJAMIN F. *History of Long Island, New York,* 1st ed. New York, 1839. 2d ed. 2 vols. New York, 1843.

THOMPSON, ZADOCK. *History of Vermont.* Burlington, 1853.

TURREL, EBENEZER. *Memoirs of the Life and Death of that Pious and Ingenuous Gentlewoman, Mrs. Jane Turrell.* Boston, 1735.

TYLER, MOSES COIT. *History of American Literature, 1607–1765.* New York, 1878.

VAN RENSSELAER, MRS. JOHN. *The Goede Vrouw of Mana-ha-ta.* New York, 1898.

VEBLEN, THORSTEIN. *The Theory of the Leisure Class; an Economic Study of Institutions.* New York, 1919.

WATERS, T. F. *A Sketch of John Winthrop the Younger* Ipswich, 1900.

WEEDEN, WILLIAM B. *Economic History of New England, 1620–1789.* 2 vols. Boston, 1890.

WELDE, THOMAS. *Short History of the Rise, Reign, and Ruine of the Antinomians in the Colony of Massachusetts Bay* (1644), in C. F. Adams's *Antinomianism.* Boston, 1894.

WARREN, MRS. MERCY. *Poems, Dramatic and Miscellaneous.* Boston, 1790.

WHARTON, A. H. *Colonial Days and Dames.* New York, 1895.

Wheatley, Phillis, Memoir and Poems of. 3d ed. Boston, 1838.

WINSLOW, ANNA GREEN. *Diary of a Boston School Girl of 1771.* A. M. Earle, ed. Boston, 1894.

WINTHROP, JOHN. *History of New England, 1630–48.* James Savage, ed. 2 vols. Boston, 1853.

REFERENCES

Winthrop Papers, 1654 ff. Mass. Historical Collections, 4th Series, vol. VII.

Woburn, Massachusetts, History of. S. Sewall, Boston, 1868.

Women at Work, Statistics of, 1900. Bureau of the Census. Washington, 1907.

Worcester in the Revolution. A. A. Lovell. Worcester, 1876.

WROTH, LAWRENCE C. *History of Printing in Colonial Maryland.* Baltimore, 1922.

GLOSSARY

Alamode, a plain, soft, glossy silk, much used in the eighteenth century for hoods, mantuas, and linings.

Arrack, ardent spirit, sometimes made from rice or molasses.

Brunswick dress, a habit or riding-dress for ladies, with collar, lappets, and buttons like a man's.

Callimanco, a fashionable woolen stuff.

Camlet, stuff of hair, silk, or woolen, or a combination, used especially for cloaks and petticoats.

Catgut, a cloth woven in cords, and used for lining and stiffening garments; also used as canvas in embroidery.

Clogs, overshoes of various stuffs, velvet, brocade, damask, worsted, etc.

Conestoga wagon, a large, broad-wheeled wagon, usually covered, for use on soft soil.

Dowles = dowlas, a heavy linen, made in Brittany.

Eyle = oil.

Goloshes, a shoe with soles of wood or leather, held on by straps, to be worn over ordinary shoes in bad weather.

Heriot, a feudal service, or tribute.

Lutestring, or *lustring*, a soft plain silk.

Mantilet = mantle.

Manto = mantua, at first a gown open to display the petticoat; then the outer mantle or cape; and finally stuff for making mantuas.

Messuage, a dwelling-house, with land belonging to it.

Morphew, a scurvy eruption.

Moth, a blemish or stain.

None-so-pretty, tape with woven figures.

Paduasoy, a rich silk of smooth surface, used for handsome garments, originally made in Padua.

Pattoons = Pattens, iron rings supporting, by two or three

GLOSSARY

attached uprights, a sole of wood to be fastened to the foot by leather straps.

Piece of eight, Spanish dollar.

Pistoreen, *peseta*, a small Spanish coin.

Postule, pustule.

Present (in court), accuse to the authorities.

Pudding (black or white), minced meat or blood, seasoned, stuffed into an intestine, and boiled.

Russel, woolen cloth of close-grained twill, very durable, commonly used for women's and children's shoes.

Seisin, completion of ceremony of feudal investiture, by which the tenant was admitted into his freehold.

Shalloons, woolen goods, chiefly used for lining coats, named from the city of Chalons.

Solitaire, broad black ribbon worn loosely around the throat, often tied to the back of the wig, brought around and tucked in the shirt ruffle.

Stomacher, ornamental girdle.

Syllabub, a dish made by mixing wine, ale, or cider, with milk or cream, so as to form a soft curd; this is sweetened and flavored with lemon-juice or rose-water.

Tabby, a plain soft silk; later, a watered silk.

Taffety, a heavier silk than taffeta of to-day; sometimes a thin linen was so called.

Tammy, woolen stuff glazed like alpaca.

Tetter, a vague name for several cutaneous diseases, such as eczema and impetigo.

NOTES

1. Page xxi. The passage quoted was written in 1645, but Mrs. Hopkins lived until 1698. Edward Hopkins, many times governor of Connecticut, had married Ann Yale. When Governor Hopkins died in 1657, she was evidently still insane, and still under the care of her brother David Yale, as in addition to a personal bequest, Hopkins left Yale £150 a year for the care of Mrs. Hopkins. The famous Elihu Yale was a nephew.[1]

2. Page 2. Although a man might be desirable in managing a tavern, a woman was regarded as essential, at least in Plymouth County. The March session of the General Court of 1663 passed this grammatically obscure bill:

Understanding that James Leonard of Taunton, having buried his wife and in that respect not being soe capable of keeping a publicke house, there being alsoe another ordinary in the town, doe call in the said Leonard his licence.

But the Court was willing to encourage a lone woman, as well as to consider the comfort of society. The August session of the same year saw the following enacted:

Upon the motion of Mr. Hatherly and Mr. Tildin, in the behalfe of the widow, Mistris Lydia Garrett, of Scituate, to have libertie to sell strong liquors, in regard that sundrie in that town are ofttimes in necessitie thereof, this court doth

[1] Winthrop, vol. I, p. 273 *n.*, and vol. II, p. 265 *n.*

205

NOTES

give libertie unto the said Lydia Garrett to sell liquors, alwaies provided that the order of the court concerning the selling of liquors be observed, and that shee sell none but to housekeepers, and not lesse than a gallon att a time.

This particular method of liquor control has fallen into disuse of late.

3. Page 12. This was the widow of Nathaniel Coolidge. On November 5, 1789, Washington wrote in his diary:[1]

We lodged in this place (Watertown) at the house of a Widow Coolidge, near the Bridge, and a very indifferent one it is.

Washington may be regarded as an authority on inns. At Williamsburg in the years before the Revolution he had usually stayed at a house kept by Mrs. Dawson; the editor of the "Diary" says that Elizabeth (Churchill) Dawson, widow of the president of William and Mary College, kept a fashionable boarding house. "The club," where Washington frequently dined, met at the inn kept by a Mrs. Campbell. As he went to these houses year after year, it may be confidently assumed that he found them more satisfactory than that of Mrs. Coolidge.

4. Page 20. Richard Copley and his wife Mary Singleton were both natives of Ireland, according to family tradition better supplied with ancestors than with money, and soon after their marriage they came to Boston, hoping to make their way in the New

[1] *Diaries of George Washington.* J. C. Fitzpatrick, editor, Boston, 1925, vol. IV, p. 48; vol. I, pp. 268, 354 *et al.*

World. Unfortunately Richard died within a year, at about the same time as the birth of his only son (July 3, 1737). We have no information about the next eleven years, but may assume that Mrs. Copley eked out a living for herself and her child from the tobacco shop. According to the records of Trinity Church, she was married to Peter Pelham on May 22, 1748. She bore him one son, Henry, who like his father became a painter of some local distinction. Fate seems to have played a trick on heredity, however, in giving the artistic genius to Peter's stepson, John Singleton Copley.

In 1751, Peter died. Mrs. Pelham's great-granddaughter wrote that he left "his widow in her humble abode...under the care of her sons." Considering the ages of the sons, it seems more likely that she took care of them; but this was written in 1882, when perhaps it was not realized that the mother of a famous painter and the grandmother of an English baron could support her family by keeping a shop! Mrs. Pelham died in 1789. In 1785 she was acting as agent for her son in renting his property on Beacon Hill. The *Copley-Pelham Letters*, published by the Massachusetts Historical Society in 1914, gives a facsimile of a letter written by her in 1784. The handwriting is beautiful, and the spelling and expression very good. It contains also a charming letter from John Singleton Copley, written in Paris in 1774, beginning "Dear and Ever Hond. Mamma." Many references to her may be found in this collection, but none, alas, to the tobacco business.[1]

[1] See also Amory, M. B., *John Singleton Copley*, Boston, 1882; and Perkins, A. T., *Memoir of John Singleton Copley*, Boston, 1873.

NOTES

5. Page 29. A correspondent suggests that the "landskips" may have been intended for watch papers, and the "ox-eye glass" have been a sort of reducing mirror which would simplify the artist's work.

6. Page 40. In the early part of August, 1772, Washington noted in his "Diary" that Mrs. Presley Cox spent several days at Mt. Vernon. His account book explains why:

Aug. 14, By Mrs. Cox, making and altering gowns for Mrs. Washington, £12.12.6
Aug. 16, By ditto, Makg. and Alterg. Do. for Miss Custis 15*s*

This activity was probably in preparation for the ball at Alexandria, on August 20, which they all attended.[1]

7. Page 49. "Sister Bradish" was probably the wife of Robert Bradish, who lived on the westerly corner of Holyoke Street, where Holyoke House now stands.[2]

8. Page 50. Tristram Coffin of Brixton, Devonshire, England, with his wife Dionis Stevens and three young children, came to Massachusetts in 1642. After a short stay at Salisbury they lived for about six years at Haverhill, and then for an equal period at Newbury, where they kept a tavern. Whether the court episode had anything to do with their leaving Newbury the following year, 1654, can only be surmised. After a second sojourn at Salisbury they went to Nantucket in 1660, where they finally and firmly

---

[1] Op. cit., vol. II, pp. 72–75.
[2] *Cambridge*, p. 228 *n.*

established themselves. Of their nine children, seven survived and became the parents of numerous off-spring. It is said that twelve thousand descendants of Tristram and Dionis can be traced, living in every state of the Union, in England, and in each of the Dominions.[1]

9. Page 142. The Pauline attitude toward women in relation to the church was persistent. In 1699 two clergymen of Salem addressed a letter of remonstrance to the Brattle Street Church, in which they found fault with its liberalism in belief and in prac-tise. In commenting on one error they expressed the conviction that "the admission of females to full church activity had a direct tendency to subvert the order and liberty of the churches." [2]

10. Page 148. A distinguished Quaker preacher was Mary Starbuck of Nantucket, daughter of the Tristram and Dionis Coffin mentioned on page 50. Born in Haverhill, February 20, 1645, she went with her parents to Nantucket in 1660, and two years later married Nathaniel Starbuck. She seems to have been a woman of unusual and varied abilities, and she is frequently spoken of in Nantucket lore as the "Great Woman." The Nantucket Historical Society owns a manuscript book headed, "Mary Starbuck, Account Book with the Indians, begun in 1662. Nathaniel Jr. continued it." Evidently Mrs. Starbuck managed a general supply store, for the account book names such articles sold as (to give the original spelling), "rib-

[1] Starbuck, A., *History of Nantucket*, Boston, 1924; Douglas-Lithgow, R. A., *Nantucket: A History*. New York, 1914.
[2] Cooke, G. W., *Unitarianism in America*, Boston, 1902.

NOTES

bining, sope, shuse, 2 scains thred," beside buttons, pipes, blankets, cotton and linen cloth, beef, and corn. There were also beverages, but only occasionally, and in moderate quantity. All these were usually paid for in fish.

Shop-keeping, however, was a mere incident in Mrs. Starbuck's life. The historian of "The Early Settlers of Nantucket" says of her:

She was a remarkable woman, anticipating by two centuries the advanced views of women of to-day. She took an active part in town debates, usually opening her remarks with "My husband and I, having considered the subject, think . . ."

In about 1701 she became interested in the doctrines of the Society of Friends. In 1704, Thomas Story, a Quaker preacher, visited Nantucket and wrote in his diary as follows:

There was in this island one Nathaniel Starbuck, whose wife was a wise, discreet woman, well read in Scripture, and not attached unto any sect, but in great reputation throughout the island for her knowledge in matters of religion, and an oracle among them on that account, in so much that they would not do anything without her advice and consent therein.

Mrs. Starbuck soon became celebrated as a preacher. She died in 1717.[1]

11. Page 157. The notice of Mrs. Osborn's benefit does not lack flavor:[2]

[1] Hinchman, L. S., *Early Settlers of Nantucket*, Philadelphia, 1896; *Nantucket Historical Association Proceedings*, July, 1915; Macy, Obed, *History of Nantucket*, Boston, 1835.
[2] Hornblow, A. H., *History of the Theatre in America*, Philadelphia, 1919, vol. I, p. 62.

On Monday next will be presented for the Benefit of the widow Osborn "The Distrest Mother," with several entertainments to which will be added "The Beau in the Suds." As 'tis the first time this poor widow has had a benefit, and having met with divers late Hardships and Misfortunes, 'tis hoped all Charitable, Benevolent Ladies *and others* will favour her with their company.

12. Page 159. Being an actor had its risks in those days. *The New York Mercury* ran the following advertisement: [1]

Theatre in New York, May 3, 1762.

A Pistole Reward will be given to whoever can discover the person who was so very rude as to throw Eggs from the Gallery upon the Stage last Monday, by which the Cloaths of some Ladies and Gentlemen were spoiled, and the performance in some measure interrupted.

D. DOUGLASS.

According to Seilhamer, the eggs may have been intended not for the actors but for the "beaux" who wandered upon the stage, "in accordance with a pernicious custom dating from Shakespeare's time."

13. Page 161. Lord Rosehill was the eldest son of the sixth Earl of Northesk; he was born in 1749 and died without issue in 1788. *Burke's Peerage* (edition of 1926) states that in August, 1768, he married "Catherine Cameron (or Mary Cheer)." It may be that Margaret (not Mary) Cheer was originally only a stage name, but if so it was used as her real name in this country, where she lived for a good many years. Apparently she married again, for she was later

[1] Seilhamer, vol. I, p. 117.

known as Mrs. Long. In 1773, after a retirement of
almost twenty years she acted in the John Street
Theatre, New York, in *The Jealous Wife*. During the
following winter she made several appearances, and
took a benefit on May 28, 1794. The public, however, showed none of its old affection for her.[1]

14. Page 162. Since the Christian names of actors
and actresses were rarely given, it is extremely difficult to disentangle members of the same family.
Three generations of Hallams, Mr., Mrs., and Miss,
trod the boards in England and America. It seems
probable that the Miss Hallam who played small
parts in 1752 was a daughter of the elder Lewis; and
that the Miss Hallam who played the lead in the '70's
was Nancy, his brother William's daughter. The
Maryland Gazette of November 7, 1771, praises a
portrait of Miss Hallam in the character of Fedele in
"Cymbeline," painted by Charles Wilson Peale.
Unfortunately nothing further is known of it.[2]

15. Page 169. An interesting article entitled *Ann
Franklin of Newport, Printer,* by Howard M. Chapin,
appeared in *Bibliographical Essays, a Tribute to
Wilberforce Eames,* published in 1924. Mr. Chapin
says that James had "the practical help of his wife"
in the printing business after he moved to Newport,
in 1726 or 1727, and that in 1732 they started the
Rhode Island Gazette, the first newspaper in the State.
It was not a financial success, however, and did not
last long. Chapin states that Mrs. Franklin became

[1] Hornblow, vol. I, p. 200.
[2] Seilhamer, vol. II, pp. 64, 138.

"colony printer" in 1736, a position which it does not appear that her husband ever held. She continued his custom of issuing Rhode Island Almanacs, at first engaging Joseph Stafford to prepare them, and later writing them herself. Mrs. Franklin printed a number of books, as well as legal forms and broadsides.

Mrs. Franklin died April 19, 1763, and the next issue of the *Mercury* contained the following obituary:

The 19th Instant departed this Life, Mrs. ANN FRANKLIN, in the 68th Year of her Life. She had a fine Constitution, firm and strong; — was never sick, nor ailing, scarcely in the whole Course of her Life, 'till a few Months before her Dissolution; nor did she ever take any sort of Medicine in all that long Space of Time, 'till that Sickness seized her, which brought her down to the Grave. When she reflected, in Health, on the Goodness of her Constitution, she was at a Loss to guess what Part would be attack'd by sickness in order to bring on her Dissolution — But in her we see an Instance of the Truth of that Word, "The Strong Men shall bow themselves" — She was a Widow about 29 Years — And tho' she had little to depend upon for a Living, yet by her Oeconomy and Industry in carrying on the Printing Business, supported herself and Family, and brought up her Children in a genteel manner; — all of whom she bury'd sometime before her Death. — She was a Woman of great Integrity and Uprightness in her Station and Conversation, and was well beloved in the Town. She was a faithful Friend, and a compassionate Benefactor to the Poor, (beyond many of great Estates) and often reliev'd them in the Extremity of Winter. — And, she was a constant and seasonable Attendant on public Worship, and would not suffer herself to be detain'd by trivial Family-Concerns: *Herein she excell'd most of her Sex.*

She enter'd into the Christian Life in her early Youth, and has, ever since, adorn'd her Profession by an exem-

NOTES

plary Conversation. And, under all the varying Scenes
of Life, and some shocking Trials laid on her in the Wis-
dom of Divine Providence, she maintain'd a noble Forti-
tude of Mind, mixt with Patience and Submission to the
Will of God; though not without Imperfection.

For several Weeks before her Death she was in great
Darkness and Distress of Mind; but it pleased God, a few
Days before her Departure, to shine in upon her Soul, and
lift up the Light of his Countenance upon her, and thereby
to give her *that Peace of God, which passeth all Understanding.*

And so she pass'd from Time to Eternity in the lively
View and Prospect of eternal Life, through Faith in the Son
of God, who gave his Life a Ransom for Sinners; that they,
and they only, who believe on Him, and obey Him, might
have and enjoy a glorious happy Life without End, in the
open vision, and full Fruition of the Author of their Being
and Blessedness.

"The Memory of the Just is blessed."

Her remains were interr'd on Thursday last.

INDEX

215

INDEX

Boylston, Sarah, 110
Bradford, Cornelia (Smith), 169, 178
Bradford, Governor William, 39, 58
Bradish, Mrs. Robert, 49, 208
Bradstreet, Anne, 126–30
Brasher, Judith, 44
Breintnall, Hannah, 28, 29
Brent, Margaret, 98–100, 186
Brent, Mary, 98
Brett, Widow, 11
Bristol, Penn., 11
Brittano, Susannah, 82
Bromfield, Abigail, 103
Brown, Michael, 44
Brown, Sarah, 44
Brown, Susannah, 148
Brown University, 172
Brownlow, James, 82
Brownlow, Kate, 82
Bumstead, Jeremiah, 62

Cahill (Cahell), Mary, 41
Calvert, Leonard, 99, 186
Cambridge, Mass., 49, 78, 208
Campbell, John, 136
Campbell, Mary (of Boston), 136
Campbell, Mary (of New York), 21
Campbell, Mrs. (of Williamsburg), 206
Canada, 8, 150
Candige, Nurse, 62
Cannon (Cannan), Charles, 45
Cannon, Mary, 45
Carter, John, 171
Cazneau, Hannah, 21
Chandler, Sarah, 188
Chapman, Hannah, 72

Charles, Robert, 30–31
Charleston, S.C., 122, 164, 173, 174
Charlestown, Mass., 73
Chase, Widow, 111
Cheer, Margaret, 160–62, 211
Cheese, Mercy, 103
Child, Thomas, 183
China ware, 28
Cibber, Colley, 164
Cibber, Mrs. (Susannah Maria Arne), 163
Clark, Katherine, 3
Clarkson, Mrs., 158
Coffin, Dionis (Stevens), 50, 208
Coffin, Tristram, 50, 208, 209
Colcord, Thomas, 111
Colden, Cadwalader, 118
Colden, Jane, 118
Comedians from London, 160
Concord, Mass., 7, 132
Conestoga, Penn., 102
Coolidge (Cooledge), Dorothy, 12, 206
Copley, John Singleton, op. 44, 207
Copley, Mary (Singleton), 20, 207
Copley, Richard, 206
Cotes, Martha, 87
Cotton, Reverend John, 145
Cowell, Hannah, 64–65
Cowley, Mary, 54
Cox, Mrs. Presley, 208
Crabb, Mary, 43
Cranston, R.I., 14
Crathorne, Jonathan, 47
Crathorne, Mary, 47
Crocker, Hannah (Mather), 84
Crouch, Mary, 174
Cumberland, R.I., 113

216

INDEX

217

INDEX

Franklin, Benjamin, 52, 77, 83, 167, 173
Franklin, Elizabeth, 52
Franklin, James, 168, 213
Franklin, John, 52
Fredericktown, Md., 12
French and Indian Wars, 10, 11, 37, 105, 130–33
Friends, Society of, 74, 76, 96, 100, 146–48, 153, 209
Fuller, Mrs., 61
Fuller, Samuel, 58, 61
Furniture-making, 51

Gale, Widow, 51
Garrett, Lydia, 205
Gazley, Martha, 92
Gee, Susannah, op. 92
George (Gouge), Nancy, 157
Germantown, Penn., 69
Gibbons (Gibbins), John, 47
Goddard, Mary Katherine, 172, 173
Goddard, Sarah (Updike), 171
Goddard, William, 171–73
Goddard, William Giles, 172
Goelet, Captain Francis, 8, 16, 17
Goodwin, Sarah, 51
Goose, Mrs., 19
Gordon, Agnes (Tucker), 73
Gordon, Widow, 21
Grace, Mrs., 17
Grant, Mrs. Ann (of Laggan), 115, 116
Grant, Mrs. Sueton, 33, 34
Gravesend, N.Y., 188–89
Green, Ann Catharine (Hoof), 174–76
Green, Jonas, 174, 175
Green, Mary, 81

Greene, Thomas, 99
Greenfield, Samuel, 111
Griffets, Hannah, 140
Grocery shops, 19, 21, 25

Haddon, Elizabeth, 100, 101
Haddon, John, 100
Haddonfield, N.J., 101
Hallam, Lewis, 158, 159, 212
Hallam, Miss, 158, 212
Hallam, Miss (Nancy), 161–63, 212
Hallam, Mrs., 158, 159, 212
Hamlet, 161
Hancock, John, 103
Hardware, 30–32, 53–55
Hare (Hair), Margaret, 91
Harmon, Catharine Maria, 159, 162–64
Harnett, Cornelius, 117
Harnett, Mary, 117
Harrod, Mrs., 73
Hartford, Conn., xxi, 104
Harvard College, 40, 49, 87, 97
Hatherly, Mr., 205
Haverhill, Mass., 3, 208, 209
Hay, Sarah, 91
Hays, Hetty, 46
Hazard, Mary, 59
Heck, Barbara, 149, 150
Hefridge, Christian, 19
Henry, Maria (Storer), 160
Hill, Nurse, 63–65
Hiller (Hillyer), Mrs., 93, 155
Hiltzheimer, Jacob, 15–16, 73–74
Hoar, John, 132
Hodges, Mrs., 114
Hogg, Ann (Storer), 160
Holmes, Mrs., 7
Holmes, Oliver Wendell, 130

218

INDEX

INDEX

INDEX

INDEX

Salmon, Mary, 53
Saybrook Ferry, Conn., 6
Scituate, Mass., 205
Scharibrook, Elizabeth, 94
Schaw, Janet, 116
Schuyler, Cornelia (Van Cort-
 land), 108
Scott, Margaret, 111
Scotton, Anne, 44
Sewall, Jane, 183
Sewall, Samuel, 62–65, 84–87,
 136–37, 183, 194
Shakers, 151–53
Sheaffe, Susannah (Child), 25,
 183, 184
She Stoops to Conquer, 164
Sherrod (Sharrat), Elizabeth, 3
Sherrod, Hugh, 3
Shipping, 107
Shotwell, Richard, 111
Silk culture, 123
Slayton, Ann, 12
Sleigh, Ann, 21
Smith, Ann, 30
Smith, Martha (Turnstall), 55–
 56
Smith, Samuel, 168
Soap-making, 52
South Carolina, 7, 119–23, 173,
 174
South Carolina Gazette, 173
Spence, Widow, 16
Spratt, Maria (De Peyster),
 104–05
Stagg, Charles, 157
Stagg, Mary, 157
Stamp Act, 37, 171
Stamper, Mrs., 164, 165
Stanwich, Conn., 1
Starbuck, Mary (Coffin), 209
Starbuck, Nathaniel, 209

Staten Island, 107
Stearns, Mary, 188
Sterling, Earl of (William Alex-
 ander), 106
Stirling, Mrs., 21
Stockton, Anne, 140
Storer, Ann, Fanny, and Maria,
 160, 163
Story, Thomas, 210
Stratford, Conn., 86
Stuyvesant, Governor Peter,
 188

Tanning, 54
Tatnall, Ann, 68
Taunton, Mass., 103, 205
Taylor, Isaac, 7
Taylor, Mrs., 157
Thayer, Mrs., 87
Theatre, the, 157–66, 211, 212
Thomas, Isaiah, 30, 168, 169,
 172, 177
Tilden, Mr., 205
Timothy, Ann (widow of
 Peter), 173, 174
Timothy, Elizabeth, 173
Timothy, Lewis, 173
Tobacconists, 20, 21
Todd, Sarah, 35
Todd, Mrs. Sarah, 90
Townsend, Hannah (Penn), 86
Treby, Bridget, 22
Tucker, Ann, 70–71
Turrell, Reverend Ebenezer,
 137
Turrell, Jane (Colman), 137

Vanderspiegel, Anna, 21
Van Cortland, Stephanus, 108
Vane, Sir Harry, 145
Vegetable seeds, 27

222

INDEX

Vermont, 61
Vernor, Martha, 11
Vincent, Judith, 113
Virginia, 109, 166
Virginia Company of Comedians, 157
Virginia Gazette, 176
Viscount, Doris, 36
Voyer, Jane, 90

Wady, Humphrey, 68
Wainwright, Miss, 160–62
Waite, Lucy, 111
Walker, Mary, 188
Walker, Mrs. Robert, 85, 86
Walker, Widow, 80
Walker, Reverend Zechariah, 86
Warner, Isaiah, 169
Warren, Mercy, 140
Washington, George, 206, 208
Washington, Martha, 208
Watertown, Mass., 12, 206
Watervliet, N.Y., 152
Wax Works, 155
Weathersfield, Conn., 133
Weeden, Elizabeth, 63–64
Welde, Reverend Thomas, 144
Wellington (Willington), Josiah, 187
Wellington, Mary, 187
Wells, Maine, 60
Wells, Rebecca, 109
Wesley, Reverend John, 148, 149
Westerly, R.I., 5
Weston, Mass., 186
Wetherell, Rebecca, 12

Whaling, 55–56
Wheatley, Mrs. John, 140–41
Wheatley, Phillis, 140–42, op. 144
Whitefield, Reverend George, op. 144, 148
Whitmore, Mrs. Thomas, 61
Williams, Abigail, 14
Williamsburg, Va., 157, 158, 159, 162, 206
Wilmington, Del., 110
Wilmington, N.C., 116, 117
Wines, assortment of, 26
Winship, Mrs. Ephraim, 80
Winslow, Anna Green, 65–66, 139, 140
Winthrop, Governor John, xx, xxi, 142, 144, 205
Winthrop, Governor John, the Younger, 58, 112
Withy, Widow, 9
Woburn, Mass., 79
Worcester, Mass., 188
Wright, Lucy, 153
Wright, Susannah, 140
Writers, xxi, 4–6, 122–42.
Wyatt, Mary (Mrs. Edward), 61

Yale, David, xxi, 205.
Yapp, Miss, 158
Yeats, Mary, 9
Yonkers, N.Y., 107

Zenger, Anna Catherina (Maul), 169, 170
Zenger, John Peter, 18, 106, 169